Functional Categories in Igbo

In the same series

FUNCTIONAL CATEGORIES IN IGBO

A Minimalist Perspective

Greg Orji Obiamalu
Associate Professor
Nnamdi Azikiwe University, Awka

M & J Grand Orbit Communications Ltd.
Port Harcourt

The Landmarks Series Publications
Landmarks Research Foundation
Box 237 Uniport P.O.
University of Port Harcourt, **Nigeria**

e-mail: mekuri01@yahoo.com   Mobile Phone: 08033410255

ISBN: 978-978-33527-1-0

Published by

The Linguistic Association of Nigeria (LAN)

In Collaboration with

M & J Grand Orbit Communications Ltd.

Dedication

This book is dedicated to the memory of my late father, **Elias Nnabuike Obiamalu,** who encouraged and inspired me to attain the highest level of education despite my challenging sight defect as a child.

Editorial Note

The Landmarks Series is a research and publications outfit founded by the Linguistic Association of Nigeria (LAN), and solely funded by the Landmarks Research Foundation. The main interest of the Landmarks Series is to publish well-written and outstanding doctoral theses on any aspect of Nigerian linguistics, languages, literatures and cultures. The purpose is to encourage the circulation of ideas generated by some recently completed doctoral theses by members of LAN. We are, however, working out modalities to extend this rare privilege to non-members as well.

The fourth edition in the series is the revised version of Dr Greg O. Obiamalu's doctoral thesis which was presented to Nnamdi Azikiwe University, Awka, Nigeria. The work discusses in some detail functional categories in Igbo within the latest model of principles and parameters syntax, i.e. the Minimalist Program (MP) whose grandmaster is Emeritus Professor Noam Chomsky.

The book is presented in six chapters. Chapter 1 is a brief introduction to the contents of the book. It gives the background information needed for a proper understanding of the concept of functional categories and why they take central place in the study of syntax. The chapter introduces the theoretical framework: Minimalist Program (MP) and provides justification for its adoption as a framework for this study.

Chapter 2 is a further discussion of the MP. The chapter starts with a general overview of generative grammar and the antecedents to the MP. It goes on to show how grammar is conceptualised within the MP framework. The economy principles of MP are discussed. The later part of the chapter discusses the place of functional categories within the overall conceptions of the MP model.

Chapter 3 takes up each of the functional categories within the scope of this study: Agreement, Tense, Aspect, Negation and Determiner, showing their historical development, characteristics and relationship with other substantive and functional categories. The chapter ends with a review of previous studies on these functional categories in Igbo.

In chapter 4, the Igbo functional categories within the verbal domain: Tense, Aspect and Negation are discussed without any theoretical inclination. It starts with a description of the verb itself and goes on to show the morphemes that mark these functional categories. The -rV suffix is argued to mark tense in Igbo, but could also encode aspectual meanings. The negative verb form has a verbal prefix which is argued not be part of the negative morpheme, but a default agreement marker which implies

Chapter 5 is an application of the theoretical issues raised in Chapter 2 to the analysis of the functional categories discussed in Chapter 3. The chapter starts with the discussion of v(erb)-movement and how the features of its associated affixes are checked against the features of the functional heads associated with such affixes. It also examines each of the functional heads and how they relate with the verb in a movement operation. The nature of this chapter demands a lot of illustrations with tree diagrams. The chapter shows that some of these categories in Igbo may not have an overt morpheme marking them, but the conceptual-intentional interface of grammar requires positing a zero marker for such functional categories. The chapter ends with a description of how these functional elements interact with one another in line with the theoretical conceptions of the Universal Grammar. One interesting issue discussed here is the role of tone in realising some of these functional categories.

Chapter 6 looks at the functional categories found within the nominal phrase with much emphasis on the determiner. Following the DP-Hypothesis (Abney 1987), the chapter shows that Igbo has no determiner in the sense it appears in the European languages, but rather Igbo has a functional element, *nke* which could optionally occur with all types of nominal modifiers. The chapter concludes that *nke* is the only overt determiner in Igbo.

Some of the author's conclusions at several places in this book are revolutionary. This is a dynamite rapped in this small pack. It is an interesting piece to read, so as to participate actively in the debates that will ensue in the linguistic theory and in Igbo studies in particular.

Ozo-mekuri Ndimele, PhD
Professor of Comparative Grammar &
Founding Editor & Fmr. National President,
Linguistic Association of Nigeria
August 2015

Foreword

Changing trends in Linguistic thinking and theoretical orientation are responsible for the rapid and tremendous development in the field of Linguistics, and especially in generative linguistics. The generative enterprise, championed by Noam Chomsky, simply dominated the linguistic scene and the Principles and Parameters approach to Linguistic analysis became the driving force in Chomsky's revolution in the Linguistic science. The most current development in Linguistic thinking is the postulation of the Minimalist Program whose basic concepts and methods were initially discussed in Chomsky (1995).

The grammar of the Igbo language is well-studied and Igbo linguists have written extensively on all aspects of the Igbo grammar. Igbo belongs to the Kwa sub-family of the Niger-Congo phylum. The homeland of Igbo is in the forest vegetation of the South East of Nigeria. The present book, *Functional Categories in Igbo* by Dr Greg Obiamalu, is a novel contribution in the study of Igbo syntax. The publication of the book is timely and quite appropriate. The author captures the debate on functional categories in Igbo within the precincts of Minimalist Program. Thus, the book is in tune with the latest approaches to the study of syntax within the Chomskyan syntactic theory. The six-chapter book, which was originally a doctoral thesis, gives a lucid and step-by-step analysis of functional categories in Igbo. The book contains a chapter that gives an overview of functional categories in Igbo as discussed in previous works. In two separate chapters, the author discusses the Igbo functional categories within the verbal and nominal domains using a minimalist framework of analysis. The book is most valuable to students of syntax and a good companion to linguists working on African languages, and within the minimalist purview.

The author deserves commendation for his contribution to the study of Igbo syntax. It is my ardent hope that the book will pave way for more publications on the Igbo grammar within the minimalist framework.

Prof. A.H. Amfani
Immediate Past National President,
Linguistic Association of Nigeria (LAN)

Table of Contents

List of Tables & Figures

Tables

Figures

List of Abbreviations and Conventions

A	-	Adjective
AP	-	Adjectival Phrase
Adv	-	Adverb
AdvP	-	Adverbial Phrase
ACC	-	Accusative Case
AGR/Agr	-	Agreement
AGRs	-	Subject Agreement
AGRo	-	Object Agreement
AGRP	-	Agreement Phrase
ANT	-	Anticipative (aspect)
ASP/Asp	-	Aspect
Ass.	-	Assertive
AUX/Aux	-	Auxiliary
A-P	-	Articulatory - Perceptual Interface
C/Comp	-	Complementiser
CP	-	Complementizer Phrase
Compl.	-	Complement
cop.	-	Copula
C-I	-	Conceptual-Intentional Interface
D	-	Determiner
DP	-	Determiner Phrase
Dem	-	Demonstrative
DemP	-	Demonstrative Phrase
DUR	-	Durative (aspect)
e-	-	Igbo harmonic nominalising prefix
encl.	-	enclitic
ES	-	Expletive Subject
EST	-	Extended Standard Theory
F	-	functional category
FP	-	Functional Phrase
FACT	-	Factative (aspect)
FUT	-	Future (tense)

GB	-	Government and Binding Theory
Gen	-	Genitive
GenP	-	Genitive Phrase
H	-	high tone
HAB	-	Habitual (aspect)
I/ Infl	-	Inflection
IP	-	Inflection Phrase
Inf.	-	Infinitive
INCEP	-	Inceptive (aspect)
IMPERF	-	Imperfective (aspect)
Interr.	-	interrogative
L	-	Low tone
LF	-	Logical Form
MP	-	Minimalist Program
N	-	Noun
NP	-	Noun Phrase
NEG/Neg	-	Negation
NEGP	-	Negation Phrase
NOM	-	Nominative Case
Nm	-	Numeral
P	-	Preposition
PP	-	Preposition Phrase
PAST	-	Past (tense)
PERF	-	Perfective (aspect)
PF	-	Phonetic Form
Pl.	-	Plural
Pluperf.	-	Pluperfect
Poss	-	Possession
PRIOR	-	Priorness (aspect)
PRES	-	Present (tense)
Pro	-	pronominal (empty category)
PROH	-	Prohibitive
Q	-	Quantifier
QP	-	Quantifier Phrase
RC	-	Relative Clause
REST	-	Revised Extended Standard Theory

Sing.	-	Singular
Spec	-	Specifier
ST	-	Standard Theory
ST	-	Step Tone
T	-	Tense
T	-	Trace
UG	-	Universal Grammar
V	-	Verb
VP	-	Verb Phrase
X	-	any category
X´	-	intermediate category
XP	-	maximal projection of any category
Ø	-	zero (null realisation)
*	-	ungrammatical
1	-	first person pronoun
2	-	second person pronoun
3	-	third person pronoun
S	-	singular pronoun

Chapter 1
Introduction

1.0 Preliminary Remarks

This chapter is a general introduction to the book. This book investigates the nature and characteristics of functional categories in Igbo. The categories examined are tense, aspect, negation and determiner. The book has six chapters. The second chapter provides a theoretical background for the book. Chapter Three is a review of previous studies on Igbo functional categories with particular focus on tense, aspect, negation and determiner. Chapter Four describes the nature of the Igbo verb and its affixes which are the overt markers of the functional categories. Chapter Five gives a more theoretical insight into the nature of the functional categories in the verbal domain: tense, aspect and negation. Chapter Six, which is the last chapter, examines the internal structure of the Igbo nominal phrase in line with the DP hypothesis as proposed in Abney (1987) and subsequent modifications of the hypothesis, with the intention of determining what counts as determiner in Igbo.

The background for this study, methodology and theoretical framework are discussed in the rest of this chapter.

1.1 Background

The study of functional categories is not new. In traditional grammar there is a distinction between major and minor parts of speech. The major parts of speech are sometimes referred to as 'substantives', 'contentives' or simply as 'lexical categories'. In this group belong categories such as noun, verb, adjective and adverb. The minor parts of speech are the grammatical elements which are not referential and have no meaning outside the grammar of the language. To this group belong items such as articles, conjunctions, case markers, number markers, tense and aspect markers. While items such as articles and conjunctions occur in English as lexical items, others such as tense markers, number markers, etc., occur as affixes.

Functional categories are closed-class items that lack descriptive content. They perform essentially grammatical functions. They include categories such as tense, aspect, mood, determiner, complementiser, negator, agreement, case and many more. These functional categories have been of interest to many syntacticians in recent times. The reasons for the interest in functional categories are not far-fetched. Functional categories provide the skeletal framework into which the lexical categories are inserted. So the study of functional categories is central to the study of syntax. Secondly, the amount of interest shown in the study of functional categories was as a result of the very little consensus reached among syntacticians on the nature, number and properties of these functional categories across languages. Welbelhuth (1995:83) notes that no widely agreed answers have been found for the nature, function and distribution of functional categories across languages. Some of the questions raised in Welbelhuth (1995) are as follows:

- Is there a universally closed list of functional categories?
- Do all functional categories exist in all languages?
- Must all functional categories be spelt-out overtly?

These and many more questions explain the amount of interest shown by many syntacticians in the study of functional categories from both theoretical and empirical perspectives.

One of the assumptions of Universal Grammar (UG) is that certain functional categories are universal. For example, T(ense) is assumed to be an obligatory constituent of the clause and D(eterminer) is an obligatory constituent of the nominal phrase. However, there are many languages that may not have the functional categories T and D marked by any morpheme. Igbo is one of such languages. It is controversial whether the category of tense exists in Igbo. While some analysts argue that aspect rather than tense is marked in Igbo (cf. Green and Igwe 1963, Winston 1973, Emenanjo 1985), some accept that tense, as well as aspect, is morphologically marked in Igbo (cf. Nwachukwu 1977, Uwalaka 1988, 2003).

Igbo, just like many other languages, does not have elements that could easily be analysed as determiner as we see them in the Indo-European languages and some Niger-Congo Languages such as Hausa (cf. Yusuf 1993, Amfani 1995). Yet, in the minimalist version of UG, the functional category D has been assumed to be the head of the category, traditionally referred to as the NP.

Matching theory with data has been a problem in syntactic research over the years. The disagreements in the analysis of Igbo syntax are mainly caused by different inclinations adopted by the different analysts. Most Igbo analysts adopt an eclectic theoretical approach which makes it difficult for them to describe Igbo data in line with the assumptions of UG. These are some of the problems that motivated the present research into the functional categories in Igbo using the Minimalist model of UG as the theoretical framework

The general purpose of this study is to analyze the morphosyntactic behaviour of some of the categories designated as 'functional' in Igbo. The categories are tense, aspect, negation and determiner.

The specific objectives are to:

a. Describe the morphological realisations of the verb associated functional categories in Igbo: tense, aspect and negation.
b. Describe the nature and functions of the functional elements associated with the Igbo noun which include; demonstratives, quantifiers, genitive tone pattern and the element *nke*. The aim is to show whether any of them could be analysed as the head of the argument phrase in line with the DP hypothesis.
c. Explain the role of tone in the realisation of these categories.
d. Give theoretical explanations for the morphosyntactic behaviour of these functional categories in Igbo in line with the assumptions of the theoretical framework adopted for this study.

There are different types of categories that could be classified as functional categories in Igbo. These categories include: tense, aspect, negation, complementiser, conjunction, case, demonstrative, quantifier, genitive and even the preposition. These are categories that perform essentially grammatical functions in Igbo. However, this work does not go into the discussion of all the categories that could be called functional in Igbo. The scope of this study is limited to the functional categories associated with the verb, otherwise referred to as the INFL categories. They include tense, aspect and negation. The scope also covers the functional elements associated with the noun. Such elements include demonstrative, quantifier, genitive and the particulariser *nke*. Some of these categories are classified as determiner in many other languages, especially in English.

1.2 Methodology

The data for this study were drawn from the Standard dialect of Igbo. However, there are many dialectal forms. The dialects that featured mainly in this work are Nneewi, Ọnịcha, Owere and Iselle-Uku (a West Niger dialect). The data are of two types: written and live. The written data are drawn from previous works on Igbo grammar. One major source of written data for this study is Emenanjo (1983) *Auxiliaries in Igbo Syntax*, from where data on Nneewi, Onicha and Owere dialects were collected. The live data were collected from different Igbo speakers especially the dialectal forms. The data from the written sources were confirmed with the speakers of the dialects. Some of the data from Nneewi dialect were generated by introspection, since the researcher is   a competent native speaker of Nneewi. Examples taken from the corpus of live data appear unmarked in the text whereas those drawn from the written texts appear with their sources in parenthesis. The reason for reliance on written data is due to the nature of this work which seeks to reanalyse some of the descriptions of Igbo grammar in line the Universal Grammar approach within the MP theoretical framework. To provide a detailed syntactic structure of the examples, morpheme-by-morpheme glosses are provided, then followed by an English translation. In many cases the use of phrase-markers (tree diagrams) are used to show the syntactic structure of the expression.

1.3   Choice of Theoretical Framework

The theoretical framework adopted for this study is the Minimalist Program, the most recent model of generative grammar as conceptualised in Chomsky (1995) and other related works. The major tenet of the Minimalist Program is the role of morphological features. These features are those associated with tense, case, agreement, negation, etc. The assumption within MP is that words are fully formed in the lexicon and associated with different morphological features. The fully formed lexical items move to relevant functional heads to check off features against the features of the functional heads. We therefore adopt the Minimalist Framework for this study based on the following reasons.

First, Igbo has a complex verbal structure where tense, aspect, agreement and negative features are marked by verbal affixes. MP provides analytic tool that assumes these categories to be seen as different grammatical nodes with their separate projections. This makes it easier to relate the complex verbal form to the different grammatical projections by assuming that the verb moves and adjoins to them to erase identical features that are uninterpretable.

Furthermore, the Minimalist Framework, unlike others before it allows additional functional projections between VP and CP. Such projection include: TP, AspP, NegP. This allows us to account for the interaction between Tense/Aspect and Negation in Igbo. The assumptions of MP and its operational mechanisms are discussed in details in Chapter Two.

1.4   Tone and Tone-marking Convention

It is common knowledge that tone plays a significant role in Igbo syntax. There are two basic tones: high and low and a derived tone the downstep which plays very important roles in the grammar of the language. Tone is very important in Igbo that some of the grammatical concepts are marked by no other means than tone. Some of the functional categories are realized as tonal prosody. This probably led Uwalaka 2003 to propose that there should be a functional category known as Grammatical Tone Phrase (GTP) in Igbo. The plausibility of this proposal shall be examined in chapter two where previous works on Igbo functional categories are reviewed.

In this work, we have adopted the tone marking convention proposed by Green and Igwe (1963) which leaves high tones unmarked and low tones marked with grave accent [`] and downsteps marked with the macron [-]. This is demonstrated below.

akwa	[H H]	'cry'
àkwa	[L H]	'egg'
akwà	[H L]	'cloth'
àkwà	[L L]	'bed'
egō	[H S]	'money'

Chapter 2
The Minimalist Program and Functional Categories

2.0   Preliminary Remarks

This book is interested in the morphosyntactic analysis of functional categories in Igbo. To be more specific, we are looking at the categories of tense, aspect, negation and determiner. In order to have a background picture of how these categories are structured in Igbo, we deem it necessary to review in this chapter, works bordering on functional categories in general and how they are conceptualised within the generative framework. The chapter is in two major parts. The first part focuses on the conception of grammar within the generative framework with detailed attention paid to the Minimalist model of the framework which is the model adopted for this study (2.1 – 2.2). The second part looks at the functional categories identified in the literature from both syntactic and semantic points of view, as well as from theoretical and empirical perspectives. Emphasis is laid on the categories of agreement, tense, aspect, negation and determiner which fall within the scope of this study (2.3 – 2.5).

2.1   Historical Antecedent to the Minimalist Program

Before we go on to expose the nature and organisation of grammar within the Minimalist framework which this study assumes in its analysis, we find it necessary to give a brief review of the antecedent models that gave birth to MP. We need to do this in order to bring out the weaknesses of these models that gave rise to the MP version of generative grammar.

The major goal of generative grammar is to account for the nature of Universal Grammar (henceforth refer to as UG). According to Katamba (1993:8), 'the human child is born with a blue-print of language which is called Universal Grammar'. Following Chomsky (1986a), Katamba defined UG as the faculty of the mind which determines the nature of language acquisition in the infant and of linguistic competence. Generative grammar tries to explain linguistic knowledge and how such knowledge is represented in the human mind and how human beings acquire language. The central goal of generative grammatical theory is to determine what it is people know if they know a particular language. Chomsky's (1955, 1957, 1965) view about knowledge of language is the ability to produce and understand an unlimited number of utterances of that language which one may never have heard or produced before. This ability is made possible by the acquisition of a finite set of rules that can be used to generate infinite number of utterances. In describing the nature of knowledge, Chomsky (1957, 1965) makes a distinction between competence and performance. Competence is defined as the implicit knowledge which a person has about his language which makes it possible for him to make grammaticality judgement about the utterance he makes or hears. Performance, on the other hand, is the actual use of the language which may not be an accurate reflection of the person's competence in the language. The acquisition of this finite set of rules is made possible by the nature of the mind which is endowed with a specialised language faculty.

Just like any other aspect of enquiry, the theory of generative grammar has developed over the years giving rise to different modifications. The stages in the modification of generative grammar are recognised by different names: Classical Transformational Grammar otherwise known as Standard Theory (Chomsky 1965, Katz and Postal 1964, Bach 1964), Extended Standard Theory (Chomsky 1970, Jackendoff 1972, Emonds 1976), Revised Extended Standard Theory (Chomsky and Lasnik (1977, Lasnik 1976), Government and Binding Theory (Chomsky 1981, 1986a, 1986b, Riemsdijk and Williams 1986) and the most current, the Minimalist Program (Chomsky 1992, 1995, 2004).

2.1.1 The Standard Theory (ST)

Transformational Generative Grammar TGG was first introduced by Chomsky in his 1957 publication, *Syntactic Structures* as a reaction to the structuralist assumptions that language can only be described from its observable surface structural patterns. However, TGG became formalised in his 1965 publication, *Aspects of the theory of syntax* popularly referred to just as *Aspects*. It was in *Aspects*, that Chomsky introduced the conceptualisation of grammar that later came to be known as Standard Theory or Classical TG. In the ST model, grammar was assumed to be organised along three major components as follows:

i)   The syntactic component
ii)   The semantic component
iii) The phonological component

The syntactic component deals with the base rules (lexical insertion rules and phrase structure rules) that operate at the deep structure and the transformational rules that give rise to the surface structure.

The semantic component assigns meaning and interpretation to the syntactic elements using the structural properties of the lexical items in a language. Within the ST model, the semantic component is assumed to operate only in the deep structure and so the deep structure is the sole determinant of meaning.

The phonological component deals with the rules of the sound system of the language and so determines the actual output of the syntactic component. (cf. Chomsky, 1957, 1965, Katz and Postal, 1964, Bach, 1964)

2.1.2   The Extended Standard Theory (EST)

The Extended Standard Theory was a revision of the ST. The major modification that gave rise to EST is the acceptance of the fact that meaning is jointly determined by the deep and the surface structures. Also, the phrase structure grammar was modified, giving rise to the x-bar phrase structure. (cf. Chomsky, 1970, Jackendoff, 1972, Emonds, 1976)

2.1.3   The Revised Extended Standard Theory (REST)

The basic characteristic of this stage of the development of TGG is the recognition of the semantic and syntactic components of ST as autonomous systems. Syntactic rules made reference only to syntactic information. Under REST came the trace theory of movement. Moved elements leave at their extraction sites traces which are syntactically relevant because they perform all the syntactic functions which the moved elements could have performed. The introduction of empty categories (traces) brought in a new way of looking at the surface structure (now referred to as S-structure). Thematic relations can now apply at the S-structure configuration (cf. Chomsky and Lasnik 1977, Lasnik 1976).

2.1.4   Government and Binding Theory

As research activities continue to probe deeper into the nature of human languages, there arose the need to narrow down the various alternative rules in linguistic analysis and also to shift emphasis from the study of rule system to that of principles. The Principles and Parameters approach which had been Chomsky's goal in developing generative grammar is formalised within the Government and Binding framework. GB is a radical revision of the earlier models where different syntactic rules for different constructions are reduced to only one rule, Move-alpha. This could simply be explained as a rule which requires the movement of an element from one position to another leaving behind a trace at the place of extraction (cf. Lasnik and Uriagereka 1988).

Move-alpha and other derivational processes are constrained by a number of principles which operate at the D-structure and the S-structure to ensure that only grammatical structures are generated by the general rule. The organisation of grammar within GB is modular. The modules are autonomous subsystems that do interact to ensure that structures are well-formed.

The levels of derivation in GB are shown below

*Fig 1: Organisation of grammar in the Government and Binding
         Framework*

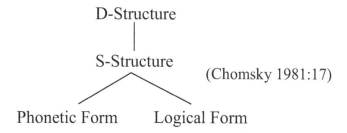

The different modules or subtheories operate at some or all the levels above. The D-structure is the base level where thematic information is represented. The X-bar theory (phrase structure theory) also operates at the D-structure. The information in the D-structure is carried forward to all levels of syntactic representation by the principle known as the Projection Principle. By the application of Move-alpha, the D-structure is mapped to the S-structure which is the level of representation where all items including the ones that lack phonetic content (traces) are arranged in their linear order. It is at the S-structure that the sound (beyond PF) and the meaning beyond (LF) are linked (cf. Riemsdijk and Williams, 1986, Cowper, 1991)

Within the GB framework, there are principles such as the projection principle, theta-criterion, case filter, subjacency, binding principles, etc., that operate within the subtheories or modules. The subtheories are listed below:

i)	X-bar theory
ii)	Government theory
iii)	Case theory
iv)	Theta theory
v)	Binding theory
vi)	Control theory
vii)	Bounding theory

These subtheories, even though independent, interact in a system of principles to define for each language which structures are possible and which ones are not, though they can operate on the same configuration independent of each other. Newmeyer (1980:76) rightly points out that syntactic complexities result from the interaction of grammatical subsystems. Each is characterisable in terms of its own set of general principles.

The subtheories are described briefly below. The X-bar theory deals with the nature and constraints associated with the phrase structure. It shows what is common among all phrases. The Government theory defines the structural relationship between the head of a construction and those categories that are dependent upon it. The Case theory deals with the assignment of abstract case and the conditions under which they are assigned. The Theta theory concerns itself with the assignment and functioning of thematic roles. The Control theory determines the potential reference of the abstract pronominal element referred to as PRO which serves as the subject of an infinitival clause. Binding theory links grammatical elements such as pronominals, anaphors, referring expression, traces, with their antecedents. Lastly, the Bounding theory constraints the operation of the movement rules.

The GB modules or principles interact with one another, as if in a relationship of mutual conspiracy, to ensure the well-formedness of structures. The principles have some variations which explain the variations found from one language to another. According to Frasier (1988:9), 'in this modular view, what appear on the surface to be major structural differences among languages result from each language setting slightly different values (parameters) for each of the various grammatical subsystem'. The 'setting of slightly different values' of a particular principle is the reason why GB is commonly referred to as Principles and Parameters Theory (P&P). It is so called because, though there are general principles which are linguistic universals, there are in addition different variations from one language to another which make it impossible to realise the principles in a uniform way in all the languages. These different variations of the principles are what is referred to as parameters (cf. Haegeman 1991:14). We shall not go into the details of GB theory since it is not the model we adopt in this study. For a detailed discussion of GB theory, please see Haegeman (1991), Chomsky (1981, 1986a), Cowper (1992), Riemsdijk and Williams (1988).

2.2 The Minimalist Program

Having looked at the various models of generative grammar that existed before MP, we shall in this section introduce some of the fundamental concepts of MP as conceptualised in Chomsky (1995) and other related works. The MP is a continuation of the principles and parameters approach to grammar. The basic difference is that the MP tries to minimise the number of principles that determine the well-formedness of syntactic structures. MP also looks at derivation from a comparative approach and the cheapest path which a derivation could follow without violating any principle wins the race.

2.2.1 Conception of Grammar within the Minimalist Framework

The general assumption in the MP is that there are just two interacting systems in the component of the human brain dedicated to language - the Language Faculty. These two interacting systems are the articulatory-perceptual system (A-P) and the conceptual-intentional system (C-I) (Chomsky 1995:390). The Phonetic Form (PF) is connected with the A-P system, while the Logical Form (LF) is connected with the C-I system. Apart from these two interface levels PF and LF, there are no other levels of linguistic structure, specifically, no levels of D-structure or S-structure as we have it in the standard GB framework.

A derivation is adjudged to be well-formed if it converges at both interface levels: PF and LF. Otherwise, it crashes. Convergent derivations must also be optimal. This means that it satisfies certain natural economy conditions. In other words, a well-formed structure must have followed the most economical path in the course of its derivation. We shall return to these economy principles in section 2.2.5. Below is a diagrammatic representation of the organisation of grammar within the MP.

Fig 2:   Grammar as conceived in the Minimalist Framework

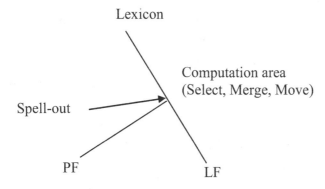

We shall discuss the labels in figure 2 above.

Lexicon

This is the pool of lexical items which the language user has acquired over time. Radford (2004:460) defines the lexicon as a mental dictionary containing 'a list of all the words in a language and their idiosyncratic linguistic properties'. The lexicon is assumed to contain an unlimited token of each lexical item. This assumption is based on the fact that derivations have to compete, and for such competition to take place, all the derivations should have equal access to the same lexical resources available in the lexicon. The lexical items are assumed to have lexical idiosyncrasies that determine their combinatory patterns. These idiosyncrasies provide just sufficient information to construct a phonological and semantic representation at the PF and LF interfaces. Ledgeway (2000:4) describes the lexicon as excluding 'whatever is predictable by principles of universal grammar or language specific principles of phonology and morphology'. The lexicon then is the locus of parametric variation. For example, [±strong] and other aspects of language variation are features of lexical items that are not predictable. Marantz (1995:360) notes that the lexical items available in the lexicon are completely formed words, fully inflected for case, agreement, tense, among other features. Ouhalla (1991:10) suggests that there are probably two notions of the lexicon, a grammatical lexicon which contains functional categories and which belongs to the domain of UG, in the sense that its categories are determined by UG, and a mental lexicon which contains substantives and which exists independently of UG, that is as an autonomous module of the mind/brain (the conceptual system). On the plausible assumption that while UG is a closed system, the conceptual system is open

Computational System C_{HL}

The lexical items drawn from the lexicon are made available to the computational system. The construction of a sentence takes place in the computational system. The operations here are: Select, Merge and Move. *Operation Select* targets the needed items from the lexicon while *Operation Merge* combines these items in a pair-wise fashion following a binary pattern. *Operation Select* selects two syntactic objects {A, B}, then *Operation Merge* combines them, producing a new complex category {C, {A, B} where C is a projection of either A or B. If B is a complement, then A projects and determines the categorical label of the new complex structure. For example, the verb *drive* combines with a noun *car* to produce a complex structure {drive, {drive car}. This is shown in (1).

(1) a.   b.

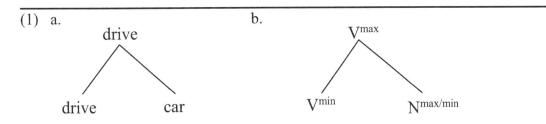

Lasnik and Uriagereka with Boecks (2004) try to explain the structural pattern in (1). They use the elementary relations in Set Theory: *union, intersection* and *identity* to illustrate the combination of A and B and their projection C as discussed above. Assume that all words have set of binary features (technically called *matrices*). For example *drive* has the feature [-N, +V] and *car* has the features [+N, -V]. If we assume that C is a union of A and B, then a combination like drive car will have the feature which is strange. C is both $\pm$N and $\pm$V. This is contradictory because it means that C is an N and at the same time not an N. It is a V and at the same time not a V. So for this reason, union is ruled out as the result of the merger. They consider *intersection* next. If it is assumed that C is an intersection of A and B and A is a verb with the features [-N, +V], while B is a noun with the features [+N –V], they do not have anything in common and so the point of intersection will be empty. It implies that C will be an empty set with no features. This implies that C has no categorical status and there is no way the system can determine its combinatory possibility if there is need for further combination. This is certainly not the way linguistic symbols combine to form phrases. The third possible outcome of a set is *identity*. When we combine A and B, the features of C are identical to either the features of A or the features of B. This is a more plausible option. So C could be replaced with either A or B as shown below.

(2)   a.   b.

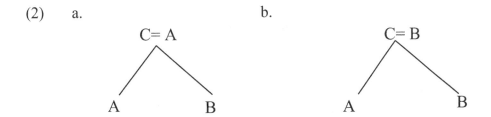

Whether C will be A or B is determined by a different aspect of the grammatical information. For example if B is a complement, then C = A which is the head. Chomsky does not see the need to represent C with a different categorial label from the member of the set that shares identical features with C. In line with Chomsky, a phrase such as *drive car* will be represented as follows:

(3)

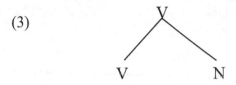

Virtual conceptual necessity does not allow the representation of the intermediate category since that level is invisible to CHL and the LF interface. According to Lasnik and Uriagereka with Boecks (2004:54), projection is simply the coding of the process of merging two categories. If we want to be accurate, we should notate X′ (as depicted in the x-bar framework) as something like {X, {X, …}}, to indicate two things. First, that X merges with '…' and second, that the result of this merger is a category whose label is that of X. This is what X′ really means.

Chomsky (1995) abandons the notion of X-bar on the conceptual ground that a head can project to another head and a maximal category can project to another maximal category. This makes room for the creation of adjunction structures in the working area. Chomsky (1995) goes as far as eliminating the categorial labels entirely in favour of a bare phrase where only the features of the lexical items are considered to be conceptually necessary in building up syntactic structures. This new idea is represented in (4) below

(4)

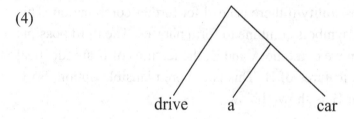

In this book, we shall retain the X-bar notation for expository purposes

Spell-out

At a point in the computation system described above, the already formed structures are submitted to the PF and LF components for interpretation. This point where the structures are submitted for interpretation is referred to as spell-out. According to Marantz (1995: 356), this point called spell-out determines which movement will affect the pronunciation of a sentence – those that occur before spell-out – and which won't – those that occur after spell-out on the way to LF. The assumption is that the operations that occur between spell-out and PF are not the same sort as those that operate within the computational system on the road to LF. What Marantz is saying in effect is that derivation moves on a path from the working area to LF but splits at a point – spell-out, where the derivation is interpreted by the rules and operations within a separate phonological component. The derivation must therefore converge both at the PF level and the LF level which are both independent of one another. Spell-out in a way could be seen as a replacement for s-structure of the standard GB framework except that unlike s-structure, spell-out has no further properties. It is not the locus of satisfaction of any conditions or constraints.

Phonetic Form (PF)

This is an interface level with the articulatory-perceptual component where the sentence is assigned phonetic representation (Chomsky, 1995:2). The form of the sentence that is pronounced and heard is the output of PF. Radford (1997: 521) defines the PF as the component of grammar which converts syntactic structures produced by merger and movement operations to PF representation. The PF representation refers to the actual pronunciation conditioned by certain phonological rules. However, word order could in a way be determined by the PF component. (cf. Chomsky 1995:413)

Logical Form (LF)

This is an interface level where meaning is determined by the nature of the syntactic form of the structure. It is the interface between grammar and the conceptual-intentional properties of language. LF is not a level of semantic structure per se but rather 'it expresses only aspects of semantic structure that are syntactically expressed, or that are contributed by grammar' (Huang 1995:15). In the minimalist framework, with the abandonment of D-structure and S-structure, all output conditions (theta-criterion, case filter, subjacency, binding theory, etc.) are checked at LF (cf. Szabolcsi 2001).

According to Chomsky (1995:2), there are just these 'two interface levels, Phonetic Form (PF) at the A-P interface and Logical Form (LF) at the C-I interface. This double interface property is one way to express the traditional description of language as sound with a meaning, traceable at least back to Aristotle'.

2.2.2 Structure-building within the Minimalist Program

We have discussed some aspects of structure building under our discussion of the computational system. Phrases and sentences are built up by series of merger operation. Merger is an MP term referring to the combination of lexical items in a pairwise fashion in the course of building up syntactic structures. Radford (2004:70) assumes that there are two universal principles which the structures must obey to be grammatical. The two principles are Headedness Principle and Binarity Principle.

Headedness Principle
Every syntactic structure is a projection of a head word

Binarity Principle
Every syntactic structure is binary branching

The Headedness Principle is fairly old within the generative tradition. Phrases are assumed to be headed by lexical items that give the phrases their characteristics. For example, the NP is headed by a noun, a VP by a verb and a PP by a preposition. This came to be known as the Endocentricity Principle (cf. Radford, 1988, Riemsdijk and Williams, 1986). The Binarity Principle on the other hand is relatively new. It came with the introduction of x-bar principle (Chomsky, 1970, Jackendoff, 1977). Within the older framework there seems to be no limit to the number of branches a node could have. For example, in Chomsky (1965), a sentence is assumed to have three basic branches as shown below:

(5)

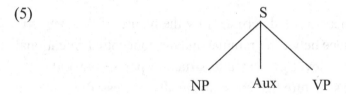

Within MP, structures are assumed to be strictly binary in nature.

MP claims that derivation has no starting point per se in the sense of D-structure analysis, but rather involves the merging of lexical items drawn from the lexicon to build up constituent structure. There are various possible derivations that have to compete for convergence and all these derivations have access to the same lexical resources. In that sense, MP derivations start from a set of lexical resources. Marantz (1995:360) explains that 'computation involves putting lexical items together and competition among derivations involves comparison of computations on the same set of lexical item'. The derivation that satisfies all the economy principles (which we shall discuss in section 2.2.5) converges at the interface levels and thus the only grammatical derivation for that set. The discussion can be made concrete by looking at the structures below, which are English expressions.

(6)   a.   The man bought a car

         b.   * bought a man the car

         c.   *the bought man car a

(6a – c) are possible derivations from the same lexical resources, only (6a) converges because it satisfies all the principles and follows the most optimal path (that is the most economical means in the derivation process). This implies the 'least effort', but if it follows a longer path, it occurs because that is the 'last resort' to ensure grammaticality. Others violate one or more principles of UG.

The construction of a sentence takes place in the working area (computational system). The working area has some of the contents of the lexicon spilt onto it. The lexical items in the working area are accessible to the computational system. It is also assumed that there are unlimited tokens of each lexical item, such that the competing derivations will all have access to a token of each lexical item and each derivation decides what to do with its own tokens of lexical items. The derivation that does the most economical thing wins the race and becomes the only grammatical structure. Others are judged to be ungrammatical. We have earlier noted that within the computational system, three operations are involved: Operation-select, operation-merge and operation-move (also referred to as Attract). These operations are responsible for assembling lexical items into larger constituents. Let us illustrate how these operations work using this simple English sentence in (7).

(7)   John bought a car

It is assumed that derivations apply bottom up. Operation-select selects the NP *car* and the determiner *a* and Operation-merge puts them together to form a DP. The DP *a car* is further merged with the verb *bought* to form a larger constituent, V′ *bought a car*. The V′ *bought a car* merges with a subject DP *John* to form a VP. The stage so far reached in the derivation is shown on the tree diagram below.

(8)

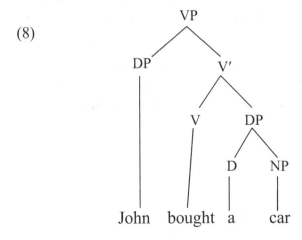

The derivation in (8) is in line with the VP Internal Subject Hypothesis. We have only shown the derivation of a VP which contains the verb with its subject and object arguments. The structure is not yet a sentence until some other operations apply within the computational area to check the tense and case features, among others, borne by the DPs and the verb. The two other operations are Operation Move and Operation Check. To derive a full sentence, further selection and merging are involved. In the case of (8), there is, for example, the need for the formed VP to merger with a functional head T to check the past tense feature borne by the verb *bought*. We shall suspend the discussion of the derivational process of our sample sentence until after the discussion of functional categories and feature-checking. The reason is that the understanding of the role of functional categories and feature-checking in grammar will make it clearer why there is need to further expand the tree diagram in (8).

2.2.3 *Functional Categories within the Minimalist Framework*

In addition to the substantive categories: N, V, A, P in the lexicon, there are also functional categories. The Minimalist assumption is that at least, C(omplementizer), D(eterminer), T(ense) and the light v are perhaps universal categories (cf. Ledgeway, 2000). Though, not every language will have them realised overtly. In the MP, they 'assume a central role since they have interpretable features which provide instructions to the PF and LF interfaces. Moreover, they are responsible for feature checking, the procedure which drives Move and, in part, Merge' (Ledgeway, 2000:10). The emphasis within the MP framework is that functional categories are more of abstract syntactic heads which may or may not have overt morphological reflexes. Their major function is to check the features of lexical categories that adjoin to them or moved to their Spec positions. C, for example, may carry the strong feature Q(uestion) which requires wh-phrases to move to C to check that strong Q feature in interrogative sentences. D carries interpretable features regarding the definite, referential and animacy properties of its nominal complement. T as a functional category has features that attract verb and DP to it. The D-features of T requires DP from the Spec VP position to move to its Spec position in satisfaction of the Extended Projection Principle (EPP), a principle that requires every clause to have subject. The V-features of T requires the verb to move and adjoin to it in a head to head relationship. Since we have started mentioning feature checking in the discussion of functional categories, we turn now to the subject.

2.2.4 *Features and Feature-checking*

It is generally assumed within the MP framework that words are describable in terms of a set of features. These features are phonetic, grammatical and semantic in nature. The PF representation is assumed to contain only phonetically interpretable features, while the LF representation contains only semantically interpretable features. If a derivation contains only phonetically interpretable features at the PF level, the derivation is said to converge at PF. On the other hand, if the LF representation contains only semantically interpretable features, the derivation is said to converge at LF. When only the interpretable features occur at the required interface levels, the derivation is said to satisfy the UG constraint known as the Principle of Full Interpretation (PFI). PFI specifies that a representation for a given expression must contain all and only those elements which contribute directly to its interpretation at the relevant level (cf. Radford 1997:171).

It has been noted that the PF representations contain only phonetically interpretable features, while the LF representations contain only semantically interpretable features. It is then left to explain what happens to the grammatical features, some of which are not interpretable, but play roles in the grammatical derivation. Words contain phonetic, semantic as well as grammatical features. Grammatical features include number, gender and person features which Chomsky refers to as Φ-features (phi-features). They also include the case features which determine the morphological form of words. Some of these grammatical features have some semantic content and so are interpretable at LF, while some, for example the case features have no semantic content and so uninterpretable at LF and therefore must have to be eliminated. The process of ensuring that only interpretable features are visible at the interface levels is what is known as feature-checking.

It is assumed that lexical items carry three different sets of grammatical features: head features (the inherent grammatical properties of the lexical items), specifier features (the features that determine the type of complement that they allow) and the complement feature (that which determine the type of complements they take). Following Chomsky (1995), it is assumed that all uninterpretable features must be checked within an appropriate checking domain and that checked uninterpretable features are erased. A head checks features of its specifier and it complement. The general assumption is that all the specifier and complement features are uninterpretable as well as some head features such as case features which have no semantic content. The uninterpretable features are purely 'formal features' (Chomsky 1995). The assumption in the MP is that lexical items (e.g. verbs) are inflected for features in the lexicon and so are inserted into the derivational tree with all the affixes already attached to the bare form. The functional nodes (for example AGR and T) are not associated with affixes, nor with any phonological content whatsoever, but with certain features: tense, case, agreement among others (Marantz 1995: 360). Chomsky (1993) suggests that features on the verb are then checked against the corresponding features encoded in the inflectional categories: AGR and T. If the features of V and that of the inflectional category are compatible, then the features of the functional categories are erased. Feature checking takes place in a Spec-head structure [XP spec[X′ X] and in the head adjunction structure [X[Y]X].

Chomsky (1993, 1995) makes a distinction between strong and weak features. The assumption is that strong features must be eliminated before spell-out, while weak features can wait to be checked at LF. Therefore, [±strong] plays a central role in language variation. For example, it determines the difference between English and French. French has a strong V-features of T and so triggers off overt movement of V to T. Whereas English has weak features, and therefore allows V to stay in-situ, but undergoes covert movement at LF to check its features (see the discussion of Procrastinate in section 2.2.5 below). An articulated clause structure with the relevant functional categories as presented in Marantz (1995:364) is shown in (10) below. On the tree diagram in (10), Marantz (1995: 364) comments, 'Chomsky leaves open what principles determine the hierarchical ordering of the various XPs ... as well as the question of whether this hierarchical ordering might vary from language to language'. To illustrate the checking configuration, let us return to thesample sentence (7) repeated here as (9) for convenience.

(9)   John bought a car

We have shown in (8) how the VP is formed by merging the verb with its argument DPs. The verb *bought* has ACC case feature to check against its DP object complement *a car*. The verb also has PAST tense feature to check against T and also AGR features to check against its DP arguments (subject and object). The DP arguments *John* and *a car* have case features and phi-features which they have to check against the head features of the functional categories AGR and T, and so they have to move to the Spec positions of these functional heads to check these features. This is in line with the general notion in the MP, that movement is generally motivated by morphological considerations. For example, the verb moves to AGR and T in order to have its morphological features checked.

(10)

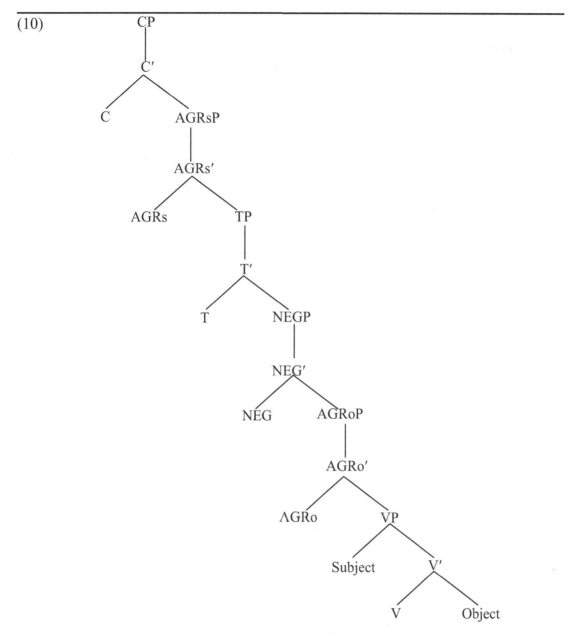

At some point in our derivation, a functional category AGR is targeted and projected to AGR′ after being merged with the already formed VP. This AGR is designated as AGRo (Agreement between the verb and its object) (Chomsky1993). The next step involves targeting another functional head T and projecting a T′ and then inserting the AGRoP which already has the VP as its complement. The next step is the projection of another functional head, this time around a higher AGR head known as AGRs (Agreement of subject). The AGRs will now have the TP inserted as its complement.

The subject DP *John* is then moved from the spec of VP to the spec of AGRs where its case and phi-features are checked by the combination of the AGRs and T (the complex head T has the verb already adjoined to it before adjoining with the AGRs head forming a more complex structure). Our discussion so far is illustrated on the tree diagram in (11) below

(11)

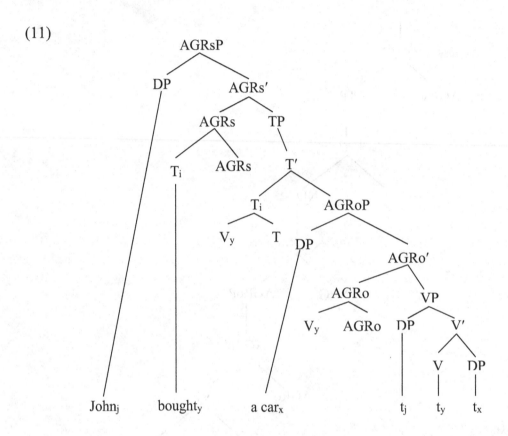

The tree in (11) shows movement operations that take place before and after spell-out. Those movements that take place after spell-out are known as LF movement (i.e. covert movement). 11 is an abstract representation of the derivation of the sentence. The only overt movement is the movement of the subject DP from the spec of VP to the spec of AGRs. The other movements are covert LF movements which do not actually show traces as seen in 11. LF movement is motivated to ensure that all uninterpretable features at LF are eliminated. In our illustrative sentence, the object DP *a car* undergoes LF movement to the Spec of AGRo to check its ACC case and phi-features. The verb bought undergoes LF movement to T and AGR to check its tense and its agreement features with the subject DP in the spec of AGRs. The case and phi-features of the object

DP are checked by the V+AGRo combination (the verb had earlier adjoined to AGRo to form a complex head). These movements are LF movements and therefore covert.

2.2.5 The Economy Principles of the Minimalist Program

Derivations are judged to be well-formed if they met the principle of Full interpretation. But in addition to that, a derivation must be optimal. The process of computation should follow the most economical path such as the imposition of locality on movement which excludes superfluous steps. These economy principles have been metaphorised in the literature as Shortest move. Greed and Procrastinate

Shortest Move

This economy principle requires elements to take the shortest step in their movement process. An element must move to the closest available landing site from its original position. The next available landing site is the one accessible to the element being moved. A position is accessible if it is the same kind with the moving item. For example, a head category should move to the closest available head category whether that head position is filled with another head or not. The Shortest Move principle prevents movement from passing over an intervening node of the right kind. A DP undergoing A-movement cannot skip an A-position to move to another higher A-position. The same thing is applicable to A-bar movement of wh-constituents. Marantz (1995:355) notes that the Shortest Move principle has taken 'over much of the work performed by Relativised Minimality (cf. Rizzi 1990), Subjacency (cf. Ross 1967, Chomsky 1973) and the Head Movement Constraint (HMC) (cf. Travis 1984) in earlier versions of P&P theory'.

Greed

Within the minimalist program, movement operations are morphologically driven by feature-checking. A constituent moves to check its features and not for that of another constituent. This means that constituents are selfish and 'greedy'. Also, the principle of Greed ensures that constituents do not move in order to check off features that have already been checked. For example, an NP in a case-marked position cannot move in order to check its case-features since such features can be checked in its base position. Such a movement will be altruistic (Radford 1997, Marantz 1995)

Procrastinate

The principle of Procrastinate 'expresses the idea that covert movement is less costly than its overt analogue' (Ledgeway 2000:14). Procrastinate prefers derivation that holds off on movement until after spell-out. However, procrastinate can be violated if it is required for convergence and still assumed to be economical. In other words, violation of procrastinate is a 'last resort' to ensure convergence. Marantz (1995:372) illustrates the principle of procrastinate by looking at the relative position of the verb in English and French. In French, main verbs do raise to Tense before spell-out, while in English, main verbs stay in-situ but undergo covert movement after spell-out. This is illustrated by the position of the VP-adjoined adverbs in both languages as illustrated in (12)

(12)   a.   Elmer lave   souvent son chat
                    Elmer washes often   his cat

        b.   Elmer often washes his cat

In French as illustrated in (12a), the verb *lave* moves to Tense across the VP adverb *souvent* before spell-out. This is a violation of Procrastinate in order for the derivation to converge. Chomsky (1995) explains the difference between V-movement in French and English in terms of strong and weak features. V-features in French are strong and need to be checked off via movement or else they will be visible at PF. In English, the V-features are weak and a delay in movement prior to spell-out will not affect convergence because the weak features of V will be invisible at PF. Therefore, English obeys the principle of Procrastinate, while French violates it for convergence (cf. Marantz, 1995, Pollocks, 1989).

      Having looked at the basic assumptions of our theoretical frameworks, let us turn now to works bothering on the functional categories and attempts to distinguish them from substantive categories. Our review from this point on will be from both theoretical and empirical perspectives.

2.3   Functional Versus Substantive Categories

Traditionally, parts of speech are usually divided into two classes: open and closed classes. Emonds (1985) distinguishes between the two classes by mentioning two properties that make them distinct. One, the open class categories which he referred to as substantives have many members and their number cannot be easily determined. Whereas, the closed class items are fewer in number, at most twenty to thirty, depending on the language. Secondly, the open class categories are so called because new items can be admitted into their classes. The open class categories include: noun, verb, adjective, adverb. In contrast, the closed class categories do not admit any new member. To this group belongs categories such as preposition, determiner, complementizer, auxiliary, tense and aspect markers, negative markers, etc.

Closely related to the distinction between open and closed classes is the distinction between functional and lexical categories. Muysken (2008:3) prefers to use the term 'functional category' instead of 'function word' because according to him, the items so designated as functional may not be word after all. Muysken's observation points to the fact that functional categories could exist in so many forms: as words, as affixes, as clitics or even as null categories. Carnie (2007:45) observes that "lexical parts of speech provide the content of the sentence while functional parts of speech by contrast provide the grammatical information". He metaphorises the functional categories as the 'glue' that holds a sentence together. Ouhalla (1991) refers to the lexical categories as substantives. The difference between the two classes motivated Tsimpli and Ouhalla (1990) to suggest that the lexicon could probably be divided into two: the grammatical lexicon and the mental lexicon. According to them, the grammatical lexicon should contain the functional categories and belong to the domain of UG. The mental lexicon contains the substantive categories and exist independent of UG. This implies that the mental lexicon is an autonomous module of the mind. If UG is a closed system and uniformly endowed in every human being and yet new words can be added into the inventory of human languages, then the views of Tsimpli and Ouhalla (1990) seem plausible. However, whether functional or substantive, the lexicon differs from language to language. Human beings do not have the same inventory of functional words. Ouhalla (1991: 10) however, points out that the views expressed in Tsimpli and Ouhalla (1990) 'hardly qualify as a basis on which one can formulate significant distinction which can provide us with clues as to the grammatical properties of the two types of categories". He rather argues in line with Stowell (1981) and Chomsky (1981) that the major difference between substantive and functional categories is that the former has the ability to assign thematic role, while the later lacks that ability. Ouhalla goes further to argue that verbs, uncontroversially, take at least one argument, be they transitive, intransitive or unaccusative. For nouns and adjectives, he argues that the derived ones take arguments just like the verbs from which they are derived as demonstated by the parallel structure between (13) and (14).

(13)   John's destruction of the evidence
(14)   John destroyed the evidence

The noun 'destruction' takes two arguments just like the verb 'destroy'. For the non-derived nouns, he argues that they have the ability to assign thematic roles on the basis of the fact that they can function as heads of possessive constructions. In that case, nouns can assign theta roles. 'The only difference lies in, that the unique thematic role of intransitive and unaccusative verbs is required to be realised structurally, while that of non-derived nouns, in fact of nouns in general is not (Ouhalla 1991:11-12). This view is in line with the views of Chomsky (1970), Zubizarreta (1987), Grimshaw (1988), among others.

Functional categories, on the other hand, lack the ability to assign theta roles and therefore do not take arguments as complement. Ouhalla (1991) concludes that a given lexical item is either a substantive or a functional category, depending on whether it has the ability to assign a thematic role or not. Ouhalla uses the term 'lexical' item because a functional category could also be lexical. Abney (1987) is the first to propose the use of functional categories as a replacement for Chomsky's (1986a) 'non-lexical' categories, on the grounds that such categories sometimes appear as independent words, and so could said to be lexical as well.

Chomsky (1970; 1974; 1986a) uses what is standardly referred to as the category tetrachotomy to classify parts of speech. The tetrachotomy uses the features [±N ±V]. Based on this, the major classes have the following features:

$$
\begin{array}{lll}
\text{(N)oun} & - & [\text{+N -V}] \\
\text{(V)erb} & - & [\text{-N +V}] \\
\text{(A)djective} & - & [\text{+N +V}] \\
\text{(P)reposition} & - & [\text{-N -V}]
\end{array}
$$

The essence of using features to identify categories is to show the intersection between categories and explain why certain categories behave alike in syntactic construction. For example, the category N and A are [+N], while the category V and P are [-N]. The categories V and A are [+V] while the categories N and P are [-V].

Chomsky's feature matrix covers only the lexical categories. The so called minor parts of speech such as complementiser, determiner, Inflection (including Tense, Agreement elements and modals) are referred to as non-lexical categories (cf. Chomsky 1986a).

To accommodate the closed class items, Fukui (1986) adds cross-classifying features [± Functional, ± Kase] to Chomsky's [± N ± V]. Fukui's proposal is summarised in the table below.

Table I: Fukui's (1986 : 55) classification of functional categories in English

	C		I		D	
	+Wh	that	T/Agr	To	's	The
(N)ominal	–	–	–	–	+	+
(V)erbal	–	–	+	+	–	–
(F)unctional	+	+	+	+	+	+
(K)ase	+	–	+	–	+	–

Fukui's proposal implies that the functors could still be described with the features +N +V. What is common about them is that they all have the feature +F. They also share certain features in common with the open class items. For example, D and N are both +N, while V and I are both +V. Each of the functional elements has two counterparts. One is +K while the other is   -K. Wh-complementiser, Tense/Agr-Infl and genitive Determiner are +K because they are case-assigners. On the other hand, that-complementiser, to-Infl and article-determiners are -K because they are non-case assigners.

Abney (1987) further modifies Fukui's proposal. According to Abney, categories are not necessarily defined by their feature compositions, rather the features define classes of categories. Since the features proposed by Chomsky cannot handle the so-called non-lexical categories, Abney 1987 proposes two major features $\pm$ F and $\pm$ N to define both the lexical and non-lexical categories. It is important to note that Abney rejects the designation 'non-lexical categories for complementiser and INFL on the ground that they sometimes have lexical entries just like nouns, verbs, etc. Abney proposes that they should rather be referred to as "functional categories' as opposed to non-functional (thematic) categories, hence the feature $\pm$F.

Based on the proposed feature, Abney (1987) divides the categories as shown in the table below.

Table II: Abney's feature specification of functional categories

	- F	+ F
- N	V, Aux (P?)	I , C, (P?)
+ N	N, A, Q, Adv	Det, Deg

From the table, we can observe that Preposition occurs under – F as well as under +F with question mark. This is because P is somehow problematic in classification. It has some of the features of substantive categories as well as some of the features of functional categories. Issues such as the classification of prepositions led Muysken (2008) to observe that classification of categories into functional and substantive can be fuzzy. This is because there are different perspectives to the issue. Parts of speech are usually classified from syntactic, semantic, lexical, as well as phonological perspectives. The different perspectives could lead to a category being classified as both functional and substantive. Preposition is a good example. Muysken (2008:3) notes that 'the co-existence of these different dimensions (perspectives) may lead to the perception of gradience'. Gradience in the sense that a category could be said to be more functional than another or more substantive than another. This seems to be the case with the preposition. Adpositions (a cover term for preposition and postposition) are most times classified as lexical (substantive). Muysken 2008:3) observes that even "some adpositions are more clearly functional than others (compare French *de* 'of' to *dessus* 'on top'), clitic pronouns show special behaviour compared to strong pronouns (compare French *le* '3s.m.ob' to *lui* 'him'), copulas are more restricted than aspectual auxiliaries". Muysken's observation indicates that the degree of functionality varies among categories that are usually classified as the same. Elements that are not so functional could be classified with the substantives. Adpositions seems to have more in common with the fuctional categories than with the substantive categories. This position finds support in the work of Baker (2003:305) who argues that, universally, prepositions tend to be more functional than lexical. His arguments are based on the fact that the number of prepositions in every language is limited. English for example has at most eighty prepositions. So P belongs to the closed class. He further argues that 'adpositions do not take part in derivational morphology, either as inputs or as outputs to word formation rules'.

Abney (1987:64-5) lists the following five properties as characteristics of functional categories.

(i)   Functional Elements constitute closed lexical classes
(ii) Functional Elements are generally phonologically and morphologically dependent. They are generally stressless, often clitics or affixes and sometimes even phonologically null

(iii) Functional Elements permit only one complement, which is in general not an argument. The arguments are CP, PP and DP. Functional Elements select IP, VP, NP

(iv) Functional Elements are usually inseparable from their complements

(v) Functional Elements lack descriptive content. Their semantic contribution is second-order, regulating or contributing to the interpretation of their complement. They mark grammatical or relational features, rather than picking out a class of objects.

Muysken (2008:62-65) examines the validity of some of these criteria given by Abney above for identifying functional categories. Muysken observes that only criteria number (iii) and (iv) are purely syntactic. Criterion (v) is semantic and a very important criterion for distinguishing functional categories. Functional categories lack descriptive content and Abney defines descriptive content as 'a phrase's link to the world' (p. 65). Criteria (i) and (ii) are incontrovertible. Functional categories in every language are always limited in number (closed class). They take different shapes and forms. Some are independent lexical items, some are clitics, some are affixes while some have null realisation. Muysken notes that criterion (iii) has three components: obligatory complement, specific complement type and non-argument complement. The fourth issue is the inseparability of the functional elements from their complements. Muysken, while accepting the validity of some of Abney's characterisation of functional categories, points out that some of the claims are not watertight. For example, the claim that functional categories take obligatory complement can be punctuated by accepting that pronouns are instantiations of the functional category D. Pronouns do not obligatorily take complements. However they do take optional complements as demonstrated by Radford (2004:46) for English.

(15)   a.   [We republicans] don't trust [you democrats]
       b.   [We] don't trust [you]

While the pronouns in 6a have complement NPs, those in 6b occur without their complement. It is better to modify Abney's claim by saying that every functional category has a complement which may or may not be expressed overtly. On the specific complement type, Muysken (2008:63) observes that the only way to maintain that a functional category takes a single type of complement is to make all these categories obligatory, even when they do not appear to be filled in. This will be at least problematic for projections like Negation, which may or may not be present (unless they are subsumed under Polarity or Force). This seems to be the idea within UG. Functional categories such as T, C and D are assumed to be universal whether they are morphologically marked in particular languages or not. On the inseparability of functional heads from their complements, Muysken argues that this diagnostic characteristic is not really watertight. He cites examples in English from Cann (2000:43) where auxiliaries could be separated from their complements.

(16)   a.   Lou said he must go to town, and so go to town he must –
        b.   Eaten shrimp, I certainly have –

If preposition is viewed as a functional category (though Abney did not classify it as one), then criterion (iv) does not also apply since prepositions can be separated from their complements.

(17)   a.   Who did you buy ice-cream for –
        b.   Where did you go to –

In my own opinion, if traces are seen as legitimate syntactic categories, then we cannot say that the examples in (16) and (17) counter Abney's criterion (iv). The traces are silent copies of the missing complements. We therefore conclude that Abney's criterion (iv) holds.

2.4   Functional Heads and Projections

Functional categories were recognised by the earlier grammarians as we mentioned above. The early generativists also recognised functional categories, but the first theoretical treatment of these categories came in the work of Chomsky (1986a) where he extended the x-bar theory to the non-lexical categories: S and S′. Chomsky (1981) had earlier suggested that the syntactic constituents labelled as S and S′ should be seen as INFL and COMP respectively. It was only in Chomsky (1986a) that the two new terms were integrated in the X-bar structure earlier formulated for the lexical categories. This implies that I is the head of a functional projection IP and C is the head of another functional projection CP. The structure of a clause is presented in Chomsky (1986a) as shown in (18).

(18)

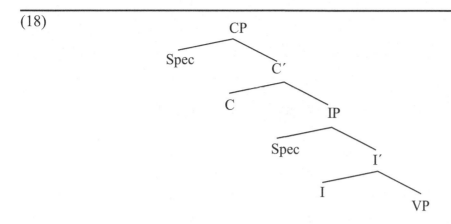

Following Chomsky (1986a), Abney (1987) extends the discussion of functional categories to the noun phrase. Abney argues that the determiner which is a functional word is a syntactic head of the nominal phrase and so the nominal phrase came to be called Determiner Phrase (DP) instead of the more traditional Noun Phrase (NP). Abney's proposal came to be known as the DP-hypothesis.

According to Chametzy (2000:17), 'a striking feature of the P&P work of the last decade has been the extension of the structuralization relation from Lexical Categories to Functional Categories, along with a concomitant proliferation (or, perhaps, discovery) of further Functional Categories'. Apart from the IP and CP recognised in Chomsky (1986a) and the DP identified by Abney (1987), so many other functional projections have been identified. Pollock (1989) suggests, based on data from English and French, that the INFL node should be split into two components: a TP and an AGRP. This has come to be known as the 'Split INFL Hypothesis'. Kitagawa (1986) argues for the existence of NegP in Japanese. Since Abney (1987), the proliferation of functional categories has continued. The table below adapted from Webelhuth (1995:76) contains a list of some functional heads proposed in the last few years.

Table III: List of functional Projections proposed in the literature

Functional Category	Source
AGRA	Chomsky 1982
AGRIO	Mahajan 1990
(ASP)ect	Hendrick 1991
(D)et	Abney 1987
(T)ense	Pollock 1989

Neg	Pollock 1989
Gender	Shlonsky 1989
Honorific	Kim 1992

The table above contains just a few of the functional heads identified in the literature in different languages.

Chomsky (1991) extends the work of Pollocks (1989) to include two separate agreement projections: AGRsP and AGRoP. He argues that feature checking (including case checking) takes place under Spec-Head relationship. The subject DP is assumed to move to Spec AGRs where its nominative case is checked by T that has raised to AGRs head. In the same vein, the object DP moves to Spec AGRo while the V raises to AGRo and in spec-head configuration, the Accusative Case on the object DP is checked by the verb. Based on this, Chomsky (1991) proposes a clause structure as in (19).

Lasnik (1999) is of the opinion that in English, the DP object does not raise in overt syntax but rather remains in-situ. It rather raises at LF. In the SOV languages, the object DP raises in overt syntax and appears before the verb. Based on this assumption, Kayne (1994) proposes a universal order of specifier-head-complement for all languages. Variation in word order across languages is caused by whether the complement moves to the specifier position or not. According to Kayne (1994:xiii),

> ... linear order can be associated with hierarchical structure quite freely. A head (H) and its complement (C) can be associated in some languages with the order H-C, in others with the order C-H. There may also be languages in which the order varies depending on the category of the head, for example, H-C when H is N, but C-H when H is V.

Kayne proposes a universal constraint on word order which he calls the Linear Correspondence Axiom (LCA). The LCA assumes that heads must always precede their associated complement position and that adjunctions must always be to the left, never to the right. The specifier positions must invariably appear to the left of their associated head, never to the right.

(19)

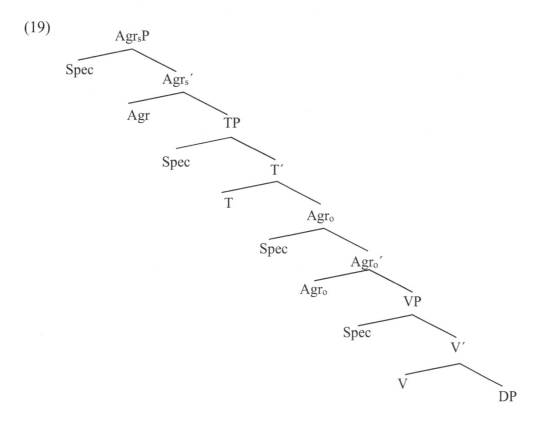

2.4.1 The INFL Categories

The idea of a node between the NP subject and the VP is not a new one. It has been present in generative grammar right from its beginning in Chomsky's (1957) *Syntactic structures*. A node was generated to host modal auxiliaries and (few) affixes constituting the paradigm of English verbal morphology" (Belletti 2001:483). This node was designated as 'Aux'. In the earlier versions of generative grammar, the aux node was assumed to be present in languages displaying a special category of modal and auxiliary verbs. English is one of such languages. Although Aux was accorded an independent status from VP, it was only recognised in languages with modals and auxiliary verbs. The standard rewrite rule for a clause in more general terms remained: S   NP VP.   It was only in the Principles and Parameters approach (Chomsky 1981, 1986a) that the assumption was generalised and taken to be a property of Universal Grammar. The node which bears modals and auxiliaries is visible in English and may be less visible (or even invisible) in other languages. With this assumption in mind, Chomsky (1981) proposes a more articulated clause structure for UG where the subject-predicate relation is systematically mediated by a functional node labeled (Infl)ection.

The Infl (sometimes abbreviated to I) is assumed to contain the grammatical information normally associated with the verb such as typically tense, mood, agreement features and affixes.

In line with the X-bar schema which ensures that all structures are endocentric (and the clause not an exception), the Infl node naturally suggests itself as the head of S and S can consequently be viewed as a regular maximal projection of I, the IP. (cf. Chomsky 1986a). The assumption in Chomsky (1986a) is that the Infl contains the features Tense and Agreement. A finite clause is said to have the features [+Tense +AGR]. On the other hand, an infinitival clause has the features [- Tense –AGR]. In other words, an infinitive clause is tenseless and consequently does not show any agreement with the subject.

We have mentioned above that in the LGB framework (Chomsky 1981, 1986a) , the INFL was seen as a single functional head with the features [+Tense] and [+AGR]. The head, I takes the NP subject as its specifier, while the VP serves as its complement. This is illustrated in (20) below.

(20)

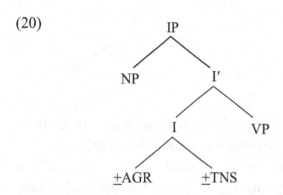

The precise nature of Infl was a subject of much debate in the late 1980's and early 1990s. Pollock (1989) made a proposal which has come to be known as the split-Infl Hypothesis. According to Pollock (1989:365),

> Infl(ection) should not be considered as one constituent with two different sets of features ([±Tense, ± Agr]) and that instead each of these sets of features is the syntactic head of a maximal projection, AgrP and IP (the latter to be called, more perspicuously, T(ense)P. In the same spirit, I will suggest that both French and English have a maximal projection NegP. Each such maximal projection will be shown to be a potential barrier for certain types of movements.

Pollock's proposal was hinged on two viewpoints: a conceptual one and an empirical one. From a conceptual view point, Infl violates the characteristics of heads which allow a single head to contain only one set of features. Infl contains the features: Tense, Agreement and other features associated with the subject and the verb. According to Belletti (2001: 484), 'a head should rather correspond to one single morpheme, if it contains more, this should be the result of the head movement operation, yielding an incorporation configuration'. On the empirical side, Pollock (1989) argues, following Emonds (1978), that the difference between the placement of negative particles, VP adverbs and floating quantifiers in English and French could be explained in line with the positions available within the clause for such placement and whether there is verb movement or not. Since there are more than one positions that could serve as landing site for the moved verb, then there must be more than one functional node. The major assumption made by Pollock is that in a language like French, V can move in a successive cycle to AGR and then to T. Verb movement to T is obligatory for all verbs in French but restricted to only the auxiliary verbs, (have/be) in English. This could explain why the placement of negative particle, adverb and floating quantifier differ between English and French. The examples below are taken from Pollock (1989:367)

(21) a. *John likes not Mary.
      b.   Jean (n') aime pas Marie.

(22) a. *Likes he Mary?
      b.   Aime-t-il Marie?

(23) a. *John kisses often Mary.
      b.   Jean embrasse souvent Marie.
      c.   John often kisses Mary.
      d. *Jean souvent embrasse Marie.

(24) a. *My friends love all Mary.
      b.   Mes amis aiment tous Marie.
      c.   My friends all love Mary.
      d. *Mes amis tous aiment Marie.

(21a) is excluded because main verbs in English cannot move to Infl thereby crossing the negative particle 'not'. But auxiliary verbs (have/be) can. In French, a similar structure as in (21b) is fine because the main verb as well as auxiliary can move to Infl. The same difference in verb movement capability could be used to explain the acceptability and the unacceptability of English and French structures involving question formation (22a&b), VP adverbs (23a-d) and floating quantifier (24a-c). The contrastive behaviour between English and French is one of the major reasons why Pollock postulates that AGRP is a distinct node from TP and VP.

We shall give a brief description of the notions: agreement, tense, aspect and negation which are the major constituents of the older Infl node. We shall equally discuss their conceptions as functional heads with separate projections.

2.4.1.1 *Agreement*

Agreement is defined by Crystal (1985:11) as "a traditional term used in grammatical theory and description to refer to a formal relationship between elements, whereby a form of one word requires a corresponding form of another to express person, gender, number, etc." In traditional grammar the term 'concord' was used to express this formal relationship between linguistic items. We have mentioned above that within the LGB framework, Agreement was seen as a feature which resides in Infl. It was Pollocks (1989) that first suggested that Agreement is a separate projection, AgrP. Chomsky (1992) made further distinctions between AgrP in the subject position and that in the object position. The two are distinguished with the abbreviations: AgrsP and AgroP. For a detailed treatment of Agreement Projection in different categories, see Belletti (2001).

Agreement between the verb and the subject may not appear overt in many languages. Igbo, for example, has no overt agreement morpheme, but Manfredi (1991) and Dechaine (1993) note that Igbo has a default agreement element in negative construction in the language. We shall show in chapter four that the default agreement is not limited to only negative constructions but could also be found in perfective and imperative constructions. Amfani (1995a) argues that 'grade' (Parson 1960) element in Hausa is an object agreement element.

2.4.1.2 *Tense*

According to Bhat (1999:13), 'Tense is an inflectional marker of the verb used for denoting the temporal location of an event (or situation)'. Lyons (1968:304) defines tense as having to 'do with time-relations in so far as these are expressed by systematic grammatical contrast'. The use of the expression 'systematic grammatical contrast' by Lyons is suggestive of the fact that tense should be overtly marked in grammar by a particular morpheme. Languages that do not exhibit these systematic grammatical contrasts are said to be 'tenseless'. Bull (1963) has a different view about tense. According to him, tense should not be seen as just a morphosyntactic category but rather a semantic category and emphasis should shift from form to meaning. Tense going by Bull's assertion should be a universal semantic category which has three possible order relationships between events and any axis of orientation. The axis of orientation being the point of initiation of speech or what he called the Point Present (PP) which Lyons (1968) refers to as the 'now of utterance'. The PP is the stand point for reference to time either anterior to speech or posterior to it. Lyons (1968:305) quoting Jerpersen (1929) *The Philosophy of Grammar*, gives a diagrammatic representation of time and tense relationship, even though Lyons himself does not agree with this philosophical view of tense.

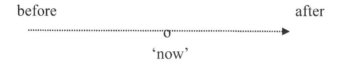

before   after

                                      'now'

According to Lyons, "Jerspersen establishes the present as contemporaneous with the theoretical zero point (the 'now of the time of utterance), the past as 'before now' and future as 'after now'. The primary distinction of past and future could be given more secondary categorisations yielding more tense distinctions like 'immediate past', 'remote past', 'near future', 'distant future' . These secondary divisions of past and future gave rise to 'seven-term notional tense-system partly or wholly realised in various languages" (Lyons 1968:305). Bull (1963) supports the semantic view of tense. According to him, the point present (PP) is the point of initiation of speech and the focal point for determining the reference of the two other points: RP (Retrospective Point), the point prior to the initiation of speech. For example, when someone says 'I laughed', he is only recollecting that at a certain point in time before the utterance, the event of laughing took place. The RP represents the past tense. The other point of reference is the AP (Anticipated Point). This is the point posterior to the point of initiation of speech. It indicates a point in the future when it is anticipated that the event will take place. Following Bull (1963), Omamor (1982) concludes that all languages have ways of expressing the three point in time and so for that reason all languages have present, past and future tense and all people have the same concept of time and order. Languages only differ in not having the same surface representation of tense. Comrie (1985:14) talks about the "deictic centre" around which events are situated. The deictic centre is the reference point. If the location in time is inferred with reference to the moment of speaking, it is referred to as 'absolute tense'. If however, the point in time is not inferred from the point of speaking (deictic centre) Chung & Timberlake 1985:203). Comrie (1985:58) takes a slightly different view of the distinction, saying:

> The difference between absolute and relative tense is not that between the present moment versus some other point in time as reference point, but rather between a form whose meaning specifies the present moment as reference point and a form whose meaning does not specify that the present moment must be its reference point. Relative tenses thus have the present moment as one of their possible reference points, but this is a problem of interpretation rather than of meaning.

Katamba (1993) observes that in the morphology of many languages, not all the three tense distinctions are obtained. Some languages might make only one or two distinctions. Lyons (1968) in rejection of Jerpersen's philosophical categorisation of tense, observes that various categorisations are possible. The 'theoretical zero point' (the now of utterance) might be included with either 'past' or 'future' to yield on one hand, a dichotomy between 'future' and 'non-future' or on the other hand, a dichotomy between 'past' and 'non-past'. A different dichotomy (based on the distinction of 'now' and 'not-now' without reference to the directionality of time) could be 'present' v. 'non-present'.

The two way dichotomy of past and non-past could be illustrated in English where only the past tense is the clearly marked tense. Lyons (1968:306) observes, 'whereas the past tense does typically refer to 'before now', the non-past is not restricted to what is contemporaneous with the time of utterance: it is used also for 'timeless' or 'eternal' statements (The sun rises in the east, etc.)'. This implies that the use of the so called present tense does not always capture an event taking place at the time of utterance. Sometimes, the same present form could be used to express an event that will take place 'after-now' (e.g. He leaves for Lagos tomorrow). Future tense is marked by the use of the modals 'will' or 'shall' but their use is not restricted to sentences pointing to 'after-now' (e.g. Oil will float on water). This sentence does not indicate an event that will take place 'after-now', rather it is an eternal truth, and therefore timeless. Since future tense is not overtly marked in English, Lyons (1968:306) concludes that future tense and present tense are unmarked while the past tense is marked. According to Lyons, generally speaking, 'futurity is as much a matter of mood as it is of tense'.

The use of a future/non-future distinction can be exemplified with the help of the following sentences of Manipuri, a Tibeto-Burman language taken from Bhat (1999:19)

(i) Verbs denoting an event:

(25) a. məhak ciŋ-də   cət-li
          he   hill-LOC go-NON.FUT
          'He went to the hill'
          'He usually goes to the hill'

      b. məhak ciŋ-də cət-li
          he hill-LOC go-DUR
          'He is going to the hill'

      c. məhak ciŋ-də cət-kəni
          he hill-LOC go-FUT
          'He will go to the hill'

(ii) Verbs denoting states:

(26) a. *ŋəsi noŋ məŋ-ŋi*
          today rain cloudy-NON.FUT
          'It is cloudy today'

      b. ŋeraŋ noŋ məŋ-ŋi
          yesterday rain cloudy-NON.FUT
          'It was cloudy yesterday'

      c. Julay-də noŋ məŋ-ŋi
          July-LOC rain cloudy-NON.FUT
          'It is generally cloudy in July'

      d. nuŋdaŋwayrəmdə noŋ məŋ-gəni
          evening (LOC) rain cloudy-FUT
          'It will be cloudy in the evening'

This language has two different tense forms, derived by adding the suffix *li* 'non-future' and *kəni* 'future' to the verb; the non-future form has past and present habitual meanings in the case of verb denoting an event, and past and present (also present habitual) meanings in the case of verbs denoting a state; verbs denoting an event have an additional form, derived by adding the suffix *li* 'durative' for denoting the present meaning. Notice that the non-future suffix has the past and habitual meanings in 25a and also the present meaning in 26a, but the future suffix has only the future meaning in both of these cases.

Pollocks (1989) is the first to see tense as as functional head which projects a TP. Since after Pollock (1989), TP has assumed a more central role in UG theorizing. According to Ledgeway (2000:11)

… besides marking interpretable features such as tense, aspect and mood, the functional category T also encodes various uninterpretable features such as the (EPP) D-feature, and the nominative and ϕ-features of the subject, optionally assigned to it as it is drawn from the lexicon for the numeration. Within this system there is then no place for a separate functional category Agr(eement) which assumes a central place in previous theories. Instead, we have an Agr-less model, in many respects similar to that which preceded Pollock's (1989) split-INFL hypothesis

We shall discuss tense in Igbo in Chapter three.

2.4.1.3 Aspect

Hockett (1958:237) defines aspect as the temporal distribution or contour of an event or action. Lyons (1968: 315) following Hockett (1958) notes that aspect unlike tense is not a deictic category, it is not relative to the time of utterance. Comrie (1976:3) following the earlier definitions given by Hocket and Lyons, defines aspect as the different ways of viewing the internal temporal constituency of a situation. Bhat (1999:43) also defines aspect as 'the temporal structure of an event, i.e. the way in which the event occurs in time'. What all these definitions have in common, is that aspect has to do with events and their structure and not necessarily time of occurrence in relation to utterance. Aspect answers the following questions. Is an event completed or still on-going? Is an event beginning, continuing or ending? Does an event occur repeatedly? These and many more questions are what aspect seeks to answer. While some languages make grammatical distinctions of some of these aspectual notions i.e. marking them with specific morphemes, many languages do not.

However, the category of tense and aspect are related in many ways that in some languages, it is difficult to separate the two. In fact, in many languages, the three categories of tense, mood and aspect are so closely interwoven that grammarians commonly refer to them as TAM systems. Emenanjo (1985:22) mentions the vast confusion in the literature between tense and aspect. According to him,

> There is considerable confusion in the literature about 'perfect' and 'perfective'. Comrie (1976:12) tries to resolve the confusion in these words, "the term 'perfective' contrasts with 'imperfective' and denotes a situation viewed in its entirety, without regard to internal temporal constituency; the term 'perfect' refers to a past situation which has present relevance, for instance, the present result of a past event (his arm has been broken) ... the perfect links a present state to a past situation whether this situation was an individual event, or a state, or a process not yet completed". The essence of Comrie's definition is that 'perfect' belongs to tense and perfective belongs to aspect. Thus English has perfective aspect and not perfect tense.

The most important aspectual distinction is that between perfective and imperfective. Lyons (1968:313) notes, 'aspect was first used to refer to the distinction of perfective and imperfective in the inflexion of verbs in Russian and other Slavonic languages'. According to Comrie (1976:16), 'Perfectivity indicates the view of a situation as a single whole, without distinction of the various separate phases that make up that situation, while the imperfective pays essential attention to the internal structure of the situation'. This definition implies that perfectivity indicates a process that is complete in itself. Imperfectivity, on the other hand, has to do with the internal structuring of an action or a state without specific reference to its boundaries. The imperfective is usually subdivided into Habitual and Progressive (cf. Emenanjo 1985:21).

There are many more aspectual distinctions across languages. Muysken (2008:58) lists different TAM categories and their hierarchy within the Infl projection. The aspectual distinctions he listed among them are: habitual, repetitive, frequentive, celerative, terminative, continuative, perfective, retrospective, proximative, durative , progressive and completive.

Hendrick (1991) is the first to propose Aspect as a functional head that projects to ASPP. But the debate whether Aspect is a universal category has not featured much in the literature. Some analysts propose T/ASP as one functional node (cf. Uwalaka, 2003). We shall look at the views on aspect in Igbo in Chapter three.

2.4.1.4   *Negation*

Crystal (1980) defines negation as a process or contruction in grammatical and semantic analysis which typically expresses the contradiction of some or all of the sentence meaning. Negation is the opposite of affirmation. In Truth Conditional semantics, the value of a proposition is either true or false. Negation is a falsification of a truth value. Lobner (2002:61) notes that 'negation reverses the truth value of a sentence; it makes a true sentence false and a false sentence true'. Different linguistic categories: from word to clause could be negated in principle, but in practice, individual languages display arbitrary restrictions (Payne 1992:75). For example, English can negate different words by the use of the negative particle 'not' or 'no'

(27)   a.   Books were given to John
         b.   No book was given to John

In (27b), only the NP 'book' is negated.

      Klima (1964:270) makes a distinction between sentence negation and constituent negation. He defines sentence negation as 'those structures which permit the occurrence of the either-clause, the negative appositive tag and the tag question without not'. His definition of sentence negation is English based. The major distinction between sentence negation is that sentence negation is the negation of a proposition. In other words, the whole clause is contradicted. Sentence negation is the same thing as clausal negation which Miestamo (2005:3) defines as a morphosyntactic construction whose function is to negate a clause. Languages have different basic ways of marking clausal negation. These basic ways are used for negating declarative verbal main clauses. Miestamo calls this the Standard Negation (SN) strategy for different languages. He uses the following sentences from English and Finnish to show the difference between the SN of the two languages.

(28) (English)
    a. Chris has slept   b. Chris has not slept
    c. Chris is sleeping   d. Chris is not sleeping

(29) (Finnish)

    a. nuku-n   b. e-n nuku

        sleep-1SG   NEG-1SG sleep.CNG

        'I am sleeping'   'I am not sleeping'

While English expresses SN with the negative marker 'not', Finnish expresses SN with 'a construction where the negative auxiliary *e-* takes the personal inflections and the lexical verb appears in a non-finite form (the connegative in these examples)'. It is not clear to us what Miestamo meant by connegative, but what is obvious is that SN in Finnish differs much from SN in English where the negative marker is the carrier of person and number inflections that identify the subject of the sentence.

Negation is a universal category but different languages have different strategies for marking negation. Dechaine (1993:466) observes,

> Negation inhabits a borderline between functional and lexical projections. In Igbo, Neg has the status of a functional head, interacting with X°-movement, but in French it is an adjunct, transparent to head-head relations. In other languages, Neg does not head an independent projection, but neither is it a phrasal adjunct, rather it is generated directly in some functional head: in Tense (Yoruba kò) or in Comp (as in Arabic)'

The idea that negation is a separate functional category was first proposed in Pollocks (1989) and popularised in Benmamoun (1992). Zanuttini (2001:523) observes that Pollock's (1989) Split-Infl hypothesis has led to 'a major theoretical innovation, namely the proposal that negative markers be viewed as elements heading independent syntactic category, whose semantic properies can be characterised as contributing an instance of negation to the clause'.

Having looked at the major constituents of the former Infl Phrase, lut us turn now to the determiner which is seen by Abney (1987) as a similar category to the Infl within the nominal phrase.

2.4.2   *Determiner and the DP Hypothesis*

In recent theoretical analysis of the nominal phrase, it has been argued that the noun is not the head of the argument nominal phrase traditionally referred to as the Noun Phrase (NP). It is rather argued that the determiner is the head of the phrase. This idea was first proposed by Abney (1987) and came to be known as the DP-hypothesis. (cf. Abney 1987, Szabolcsi 1987, Longobardi 2004)

Abney (1987) gives some theoretical as well as empirical reasons why the functional category D, rather than the lexical category N, should be seen as the head of the argument nominal phrase. This is comparable to the earlier analysis where the predicate is assumed to be headed by a functional category I(nflection) which takes a VP as its complement (Chomsky 1986). The DP-hypothesis assumes a nominal phrase to have the structure below.

(30)

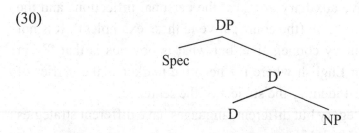

The structure in (30) implies that the D head takes an NP as its complement as well as making provision for a specifier position that could house some other elements such as a possessor argument DP.

On theoretical grounds, Abney (1987) argues that the assumption that the determiner occupies the Spec NP position is inconsistent with the X-bar principle and a violation of the Modifier Maximality Constraint (MMC), which states that "every non-headed term in the expansion of a rule must itself be a maximal projection of some category" Stowell (1981: 70). The determiner in the NP-analysis is neither seen as a maximal projection nor the head of the containing maximal projection, NP.

Another argument given by Abney (1987) in support of the DP-hypothesis is that in some languages, for example, English, there is a parallel between the structure of sentences and that of nominal phrases as shown in 31.

(31)   a.   [s John bought a car]
        b.   [NP John's buying a car] caused his downfall

(32)

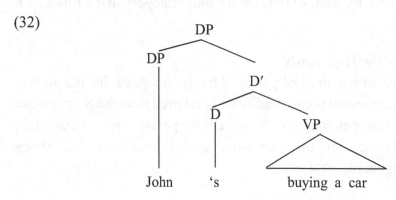

The DP 'John' is the subject of the higher DP which is headed by the genitive marker ''s' and takes the VP, 'buying a car' as its complement.

That some languages exhibit some kind of agreement between the possessor and the possessed (technically referred to as possessum) provides further argument in support of the DP-hypothesis. The examples below, from Hungarian, taken from Szabolcsi (1987:20), illustrate the point.

(33)   a.   az en kalap-om
              the 1.NOM hat-1Sg
              'my hat'

        b.   a te   kalap-od
              the 2.NOM hat-2Sg
              'your hat'

        c.   a Peter kalap-ja
              the Peter   hat-3Sg
              'Peter's hat'

The NP *kalap* takes different agreement suffixes depending on the possessor NP. Such an agreement relationship can only be licensed by a functional category. The affixes are instances of the functional category D in the Hungarian data in (33).

The DP-hypothesis provides a better framework for the analysis of the pronoun which is obscured under the NP-analysis. Pronouns are used in place of nouns. Most personal pronouns overtly show the phi-features (number, person and gender) normally associated with agreement. Obviously, pronouns are functional categories. In English, Radford (2004:44) refers to pronouns as 'pronominal determiners', while he refers to the articles, demonstratives and quantifiers as 'prenominal determiners'

Adopting the DP-hypothesis, simple nominal phrases such as 'the book' will be re-analysed as in (34).

(34)

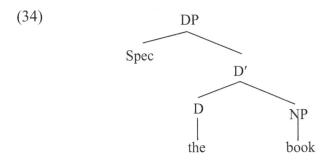

In English, 'the' could be replaced with some other elements such as 'a' 'that' 'this' 'those' 'these' 'every' etc. Their co-occurrence with 'the' is barred and this could explain why they are all classified as determiners in English. However, there are languages where these items could co-occur with the article such as in Hungarian, Javanese and Italian (taken from Progovac, 1995:82)

(35) a. ez   a   haz   (Hungarian)
          this the house
          'this house'

      b. ika   n   anak   (Javanese)
          this the boy
          'this boy '

      c. la   mia penna   (Italian)
          the my   pen
          'my pen'

The co-occurrence of the article with other elements like demonstratives, possessives, etc., in many unrelated languages led Gusti (1992) to conclude that they occupy specifier positions, not head of DP. Going by the MMC (Stowell 1981), every modifier whether specifier or complement is a separate maximal projection. Gusti's idea gave rise to more functional projections within the nominal phrase: DemP, PossP, QP, NumP etc.

Davies and Dresser (2005) argue that in Javanese and Madurese where the Noun, most times, occurs as the leftmost item within the DP. According to them, 'The distribution of the N with respect to the other elements within the DP suggests a high position for N within the DP at Spell-Out'. But they go further to argue that since D has scope over NP and therefore should be high up in the structure than NP, the left-peripheral N heads must have moved into their surface position. They proposed two possibilities: NP moving to the Spec of DP or N head adjoining to D head. They argue that the latter holds for Javanese and Madurese where the category D occurs as a suffix to the Noun. 36a is a sentence from Javanese and 36b is the derivational structure proposed by Davies and Dresser for the Subject DP *kucing-é*.

(36)   a.   Kucing-é nyolong iwak
            cat-DEF AV.steal fish
            'the cat stole (some) fish'

b.

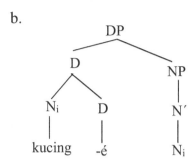

While Javanese and Madurese may have determiner in form of noun suffix, there are many languages that lack overt determiners, neither in form of definite articles and the type of determiners we find in English and other European languages nor as affixes as we see in Javanese and Madurese. Progovac (1995) argues for a D head in Serbian-Croatian (SC), a language without determiner. He uses three arguments to support the the existence of D in SC. The first one is the 'noun/pronoun asymmetries which are best captured by placing pronoun in D position (cf. Postal, 1969 and Longobardi, 1994), and nouns in N position' (p. 82-83). The second argument is that SC has morphological elements within the nominal phrase that suggests a functional head above NP. He also mentions that there is evidence in SC that shows that pronouns are generated in N, and then moves to D. Suh (2005) argues that Korean nominal phrases must not obligatorily be dominated by DPs. In comparing Korean with English where elements designated as determiners do not co-occur, she concludes that since Genitive clitic, Demonstratives, and Quantifiers can co-occur in Korean nominal phrase, then they are separate projections that have different structural representations. Furuya (2008) supports the DP hypothesis for Japanese 'bare' noun phrases. He bases his argument on the ability of Japanese nouns to mark definiteness/specificity without overt determiners and the inability of the co-ordinating conjunction *to* to 'coordinate bare NPS when they refer to different individuals'. For details of the arguments, see Furuya (2008) and Fukui (1986).

Since Abney (1987), different analysts, working on different languages have argued for or against the DP hypothesis. Languages with double or multiple determiner nominal constructions (cf. Hausa; Amfani 1995b, Italian; Giorgi and Longobardi 1991) may present some problems for the DP hypothesis. However, those for it (at least among the generativist), far outnumbered those against it. In most current literature, a nominal phrase is designated as DP not minding whether a D head is present or not. It is assumed that where it is absent, it has a zero realisation.

2.5 Summary

In this chapter, we have done a review of works bordering on functional categories in general with particular attention on how these functional categories are concieved within the theoretical framework adopted for this study – the Minimalist Program. We reviewed literature on different functional categories, especially the components of the older Infl, both from theoretical and empirical perspectives.

From the literature, functional categories are seen as closed class items which could take different forms: affix, lexical, pitch, or null. In the latter versions of the P&P model, they are seen as separate heads with separate projections such as AGRP, TP, NEGP, DP. Within the Minimalist Program, they are concieved as abstract heads whose major task is to check the features associated with the substantive categories such as nouns and verbs. The functional heads are not nodes where affixes are generated but nodes that check the features of the affixes attached to the substantive categories.

In the chapter that follows immediately, we shall examine some of the works done on Igbo functional categories.

Chapter 3
Previous Studies on the Igbo Functional Categories

3.0 Preliminaries

A sizeable number of works have been done on different aspects of Igbo functional categories especially the verbal inflectional categories. Virtually every work on Igbo grammar has sections dedicated to the description of the verb and its associated inflections: tense, aspect, mood and negation. Majority of these works study the Igbo functional categories only from a descriptive point of view. Such works include Green and Igwe (1963), Winston (1973), Emenanjo (1978, 1985), Onukawa (1994), to mention but a few. Only very few follow one particular theoretical framework or the other in their analysis. For example, Mbah (1999) describes the structure of the Igbo inflectional categories using the x-bar theory as conceived within the Government and Binding theory.

We are not going to present a chronological author-by-author review of significant literature on Igbo functional categories. Rather, we shall discuss the functional categories that fall within the scope of this study and in so doing highlight the views of different Igbo analysts on the categories.

3.1 On Tense and Aspect in Igbo

Majority of the linguists, who have worked on different aspects of the Igbo grammar are of the opinion that tense is not explicitly marked in Igbo. According to them, aspect rather than tense is marked in Igbo. To this school of thought belong works like Emenanjo (1978, 1980, 1985), Welmers and Welmers (1968), Igwe (1973), Green and Igwe (1963) and Williamson (1978, 1980). However, there are some who recognize the morphological marking of the category of tense and to this school belongs works like Nwachukwu (1976) and Uwalaka (1988). It is not surprising that there is this disagreement because the category of tense and that of aspect are so interwoven in many languages that it is difficult to keep the two apart. Nwachukwu (1976) and Uwalaka (1988) recognise rV suffix[2] as a past tense marker. The rV (past) recognised by Nwachukwu and Uwalaka is analysed as a factative marker by those linguists who are opposed to the existence of tense in Igbo. According to Welmers and Welmers (1968:75-6) quoted in Emenanjo (1985:120), the rV suffix.

---

[2] There are different types of rV suffixes in Igbo. See Green and Igwe 1963, Nwachukwu 1977, Uwalaka 1988 and Onukawa 1994 for the details of the distinctions.

... is translated by an English 'past' and the Igbo construction has commonly been given the same name. This is a misleading name, however, since for a number of other verbs the same construction is translated by an English present ... it is not <u>time</u> that is the primary emphasis in Igbo. This construction rather refers to the most natural or obvious <u>fact</u> about the particular verb used; for this reason the construction is labeled 'factative'. For some verbs, largely those with a descriptive meaning or referring to a situation, the observed fact is that the description is true or that the situation does exist; for such verbs, the factitive refers to the present. But for many (probably most), the observed fact is what happened; for such verbs, the factative refers to the past. We do not talk about 'tense' in Igbo because tenses are supposed to have something to do with time.

While we agree with Welmers and Welmers (1968) that the rV suffix marks factativity, we disagree with them in not recognising the category of tense in Igbo. Uwalaka (1988) holds a contrary view. She observes that the rV (past) suffix can co-occur with what she calls the rV (assertive). Nwachukwu (1977) refers to this same suffix as rV (stative) with a present reading. The rV (assertive) seems to be the same with the rV (factative) identified in Welmers and Welmers (1968). The rV (past) and rV (assertive) can co-occur as demonstrated by the data 1-2 from Ezinaihite Mbaise dialect (Uwalaka 1988: 52-53).

(1)   a.   Ọhịa à   r̃è-r̃è   ọkhụ
           bush this burn-rV(ASS) fire
           'This bush is burnt'

      b.   Ọhịa à   r̃è-e-r̃è[3]   ọkhụ akha
           bush this burn-rV(ASS)-rV(PAST) fire   last year
           'This bush is burnt last year'

(2)   a.   Àdha mà-r̃à   mmā
           Adha   be beautiful-rV(ASS) beauty
           'Adha is beautiful'

      b.   Àdha mà-à-r̃à   mmā
           Adha   be beautiful-rV(ASS)-rV(PAST) beauty
           'Adha was beautiful'

---

[3] The 'r' of the first rV suffix is deleted when two rV suffixes co-occur. This seems to be an obligatory morphophonemic rule in Igbo.

The presence of double rVs in (1b) and (2b) shows that past tense is morphologically marked with an rV suffix in some dialects of Igbo. That is, on the assumption that the first rV marks factativity. Even though Green and Igwe (1963) belong to the school of thought that argues that tense does not exist in Igbo, they recognise two types of rV suffixes in Igbo. They call them '-ra (time)' suffix and '-ra (non-time)' suffix. According to them, 'the –ra (time) suffix gives, typically, a past time meaning, but its meaning varies to some extent according to the construction in which it occurs' (p.54). Green and Igwe do not recognise Igbo suffixes in general as inflectional. They argue that the suffixes are lexical and should be viewed as compounds. According to them, it is difficult to find 'any clear formal distinction between compound verbs (verb plus verb) and verb plus suffix' (p.53). Based on their non-recognition of suffix as inflectional, they conclude that –ra (time) suffix does not mark tense. According to them:

> As to the meaning of the suffixes, it should be noted that those with a time meaning often supply the verb form with the time distinctions which are absent from the verb forms themselves and which forms we not call "tenses". Very many other meanings are added to the verb form by the suffixes, among which the time meanings take their place (p. 54)

Onukawa (1994), while looking at different rV suffixes in Igbo, identifies four types of rV suffixes. He identifies one as derivational, two as inflectional and one as extensional. Onukawa, following Winston (1973), differentiated the rV suffixes with numeral subscripts: rV_1, rV_2, rV_3 and rV_4. His rV4 is a derivational suffix as in (3) (adapted from Onukawa 1994:20).

(3) a. à-sị̀-rị̀   from   sị
         pref-say-rV   'say'
         'gossip'

     b. è-kpe-re   from   kpe
         pref-pray-rV   'pray'
         'prayer'

     c. o-bu-ru   from   bu
         pref-carry-rV   'carry'
         'porter'

Onukawa's rV_3 is extensional. It has been referred to as prepositional, benefactive and applicative by different analysts. This suffix can co-occur with another rV suffix (4a), or alone (4b).

(4) a. O gbù-ù-rù   m̀ ọ̀kụkọ̀
         3S kill-rV(appl)-rV(Ass) 1S fowl
         'S/He killed a fowl for me'

     b. Gbù-o-rụ   m ọkụkọ̀
         kill-OVS-rV(appl) 1S fowl
         'Kill a fowl for me'

We are then left with Onukawa's rV₁ and rV₂ which he takes to be inflectional. According to him: 'The rV₁ is an inflectional suffix. It indicates the fact expressed by the verb. It is not a tense marker and it is doubtful that it marks aspect'(p.28). It is this same suffix that Welmers and Welmers (1968) refers to as rV(factative), Emenanjo (1978) as rV(indicative) and Uwalaka (1988) as rV(assertive). The reason behind viewing this rV suffix as non-tense marker is because it could occur with verbs with different tense readings. Consider (5).

(5) a.   Òbi gbù-rù òke
          Obi kill-rV rat
          'Obi killed a rat'

     b.   Àda jọ̀-rọ̀ njọ
          Ada be ugly-rV ugliness
          'Ada is ugly'

While (5a) has a past time reading, (5b) has a present time reading. Nwachukwu (1977) recognises the rV in (5a) as different from that in (5b). He refers to the rV in (5a) as 'past' and that in (5b) as 'stative present'. Onukawa (1994:28) describes his rV₂ as an inflectional suffix which 'indicates a past time previous to another'. His data illustrating this suffix correspond to Uwalaka's rV(past) shown in (1) and (2) above.

    Almost all the analysts are agreed that there is an rV suffix that marks past. They only differ in the nomenclature. Green & Igwe (1963) and Onukawa (1994) refer to the suffix as past time marker without mentioning whether it is tense or aspectual. Emenanjo (1985) describes it as aspectual, while Nwachukwu (1977) and Uwalaka (1988, 2003) describe it as tense. The time/tense/aspect distinction becomes more complicated when we look at the other dialects of Igbo. In Ọnịcha, Nneewi and other related dialects of Igbo, there is a –bụ suffix which also indicates past and can co-occur with the rV suffix. The examples below are adapted from Onukawa (1994:25).

(6) a.   O gbù-bụ̀-lụ̀   òke
          3S kill-*bụ-rV*   rat
          'S/He used to kill a rat'

   b.   Ọ fụ̀-bụ̀-lụ̀   egō
        3S see-*bụ-rV*   money
        'S/He used to see money'

   c.   Ọ mà-bụ̀-lụ̀   mmā
        3S be.beautiful-*bụ-rV* beauty
        'She used to be beautiful'

Onukawa contends that the suffix –bụ corresponds to his rV₂ which also marks previous time. Emenanjo (1979:15) believes that the suffix *–bụ* could have derived from the noun m̀bụ as illustrated in (7) below.

(7)   O gbu-lụ oke (na) mbụ
       3S kill-rV rat   at   first
       'S/He killed a rat before'

Dechaine (1993) also supports the view that *–bụ* is derived from *mbụ*. She notes that *–bụ* is a 'V° adjunct'. This is a way of saying that *- bụ* adjoins to the verb to form a complex head in the lexicon. Dechaine (1993:477) gives the derivational structure below for the *–bụ* suffix in Nneewi.

(8)

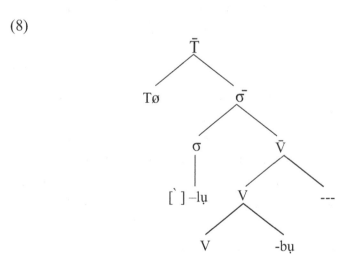

Dechaine argues for a category σ, which could be negative or affirmative. She argues that, in Nneewi Igbo (and by extension other dialects of Igbo), when σ is affirmative, it is marked by *–lụ* (*-rV* in Standard Igbo) suffix. But when σ is negative, it is marked by *–họ* (*-ghi* in Standard Igbo) suffix. (8) shows that *–bụ* attaches to the V head. The complex V head can take any of the σ suffixes. The sentences in (9) are illustrative.

(9)   a.   Ọ zà-bụ̀-lụ̀   ụnọ̀
            3S sweep-PRIOR-AFFIRM house
            'S/He swept the house'

b.   Ọ   za-bụ̀-họ̀   ụnọ̀
      3S sweep-PRIOR-NEG house
      'S/He did not sweep the house'

Dechaine argues that the *-bụ* suffix marks 'priorness' which is the same as Onukawa's 'previous past'

Of all the works reviewed above, only Dechaine (1993) did theoretical analyses of Igbo verbal inflections. Most of the descriptive works mentioned above, with the exception of Nwachukwu (1977) and Uwalaka (1988, 2003), are of the opinion that aspect is the relevant category for describing Igbo verbal inflections. It is only Dechaine (1993), adopting a theoretical approach, that recognises Tense as a grammatical category. She however, agrees with others that tense is not morphologically marked in Igbo and she therefore posits a zero (ø) T head for Igbo. This is shown in (8) above.

Mbah (1999) is another work that analyses the Igbo verbal inflections from a theoretical perspective. Mbah (1999) uses x-bar syntax as concieved within the Government and Binding framework to analyse the Igbo Infl. According to him, the Igbo Infl has Tone, Tense, Modal, Agr and Negation as its components. He claims that the major contribution of his work is the treatment of tone as a generative node within the Infl structure. Ikegwuonu (2008) follows Mbah (1999) in analysing tone as being generated under Infl. It is not clear from their analyses whether they view these subcomponents of Infl as separate heads with separate projections in line with Pollocks (1989) or as features in line with Chomsky (1981, 1986). Even though the tree diagrams presented in Mbah (1999) suggest analysis in line with Pollock's (1989) split-Infl hypothesis, there is still the IP occurring together with nodes like AGRP, NEGP, TNP (Tone Phrase). The introduction of TNP is also questionable. As important as tone is in Igbo syntax, it does not seemed justified to posit tone as an independent functional head. This is because tone is a morphological reflex or overt realization of different functional-semantic notions. Tone could mark different types of syntactic constructions. It could mark tense and aspect, negation, genitive relation by N-N constructions, question, etc. It seems to me that tone is a feature of other functional heads. For example, tone in C gives the sentence its force either as declarative, interrogative or imperative. Tone in AGR marks different constructions within the clause structure. Tone within the NP marks associative and possessive constructions. Tone is, therefore the overt realization of different functional categories. Going by the minimalist assumptions that only interpretable features are visible at LF (cf. Chomsky, 1995), we argue that tone is not interpretable. Just as affixes are not interpretable. What are interpretable are the categories that they mark such as tense, aspect, negation, interrogation, possession, etc. These categories may be affixally marked or tonally marked or may be marked without any overt morphological reflex. In recent theorizing, it is even argued that nodes such as AGR are not necessarily present at LF and should be done away with in UG (See

Ledgeway 2000). Muysken (2008:58) observes that the proposals for different functional categories in human languages is motivated by two factors. One is semantics: 'the need to link a range of semantic and pragmatic distinctions to specific functional heads in the syntactic tree corresponding to diverse constituents'. Two is word order: 'the need for landing sites for a variety of constituents that can move to the left periphery of the clause'. Tone in Igbo marks different semantic notions already captured by different functional categories and tone does not provide any additional landing site for movement. We therefore do not see any justification for the treatment of tone in Mbah (1999) as a separate functional projection in Igbo. Our position is that tone is a feature of other functional categories in Igbo and not a separate functional projection.

It is surprising that Mbah (1999) does not mention Aspect as one of the components of his Igbo Infl, despite the fact that the majority of the previous analysts of Igbo verbal inflection are of the opinion that Aspect rather than Tense is the dominant grammatical category in Igbo. Unless he probably uses Tense as a cover term for tense and aspect.

In this study we are assuming a separate projection for tense and a separate projection for aspect.

3.2 On Negation in Igbo

Most previous studies on Igbo verbal inflection handle negation as one of the inflectional categories. Emenanjo (1985) identifies different negation marking strategies. Negation is marked in Igbo by:

i.   affixes
ii.   inherently negative auxiliary verbs
iii.   tone pattern

Ndimele (2009) adds 'contrastive focus' as the fourth negation marking strategy in Igbo. All analysts identified *-ghi* and its dialectal variants as the general negative marker. Emenanjo (1985) divides the negative suffixes into two: imperative negative *–la* and the non-imperative negative *-ghi* and its numerous dialectal variants such as *-họ* (Nneewi), *-shọ* Igbouzo, *-rọ* (Onicha) *-ra/-re* (Awka), *hụ* (Owere), V (Echie). Ndimele (2009) notes that the general negative marker in Echie is a harmonising vowel copied from the verb root. He explains that in Echie, the V negative marker 'co-occurs only with auxiliary verbs or copulative (linking) verbs'. He argues further that the V suffix could have been derived from the standard general negative marker *–ghi*, but has been reduced to a vowel alone in Echie. The vowel then cliticized to the verb.

Most analysts identified *–beghi* as the negative perfective marker. (cf. Ndimele 2004, 2009, Emenanjo 1978, 1985, Dechaine 1993).

The only area of disagreement on Igbo negation is on the role of the e-harmonising prefix found in Igbo negative constructions. Emenanjo (1981), Clark (1989) and Uwalaka (2003) treat the prefix as part of a discontinuous negative morpheme comparable to French *ne ... pas*. Uwalaka (2003:12) argues that the prefix is deleted when the subject NP is one of the singular pronouns. She did not explain why the prefix has to be deleted after singular pronouns. She failed to mention that such pronouns are clitics (they are phonologically dependent on the adjacent verbal element). Dechaine (1993) does not agree with the template view of Igbo negation. She rather argues that the *e-* prefix in negative constructions is a 'default agreement' marker which surfaces as a result of stranded tense. According to Dechaine, 'Neg between T and V is a barrier for V to T movement. As V can't raise beyond Neg, T above Neg is empty'. The *e-* prefix surfaces in the Agr head position to give support to the empty T position which has strong tense features.

Obiamalu (2006) provides further evidence in support of Dechaine's analysis of e- prefix as a default agreement element. Obiamalu, however, adds that the high tone borne by the prefix is a negative marker. He concludes that high tone is the more important negative marker than the negative suffix. This is contrary to Emenanjo's (1985) and Ndimele's (2004, 2009) view that negation in Igbo is marked by a floating low tone.

3.3 On the Nature and Function of Determiner in Igbo

Emenanjo (1978:79) identifies different elements that could be found within the Igbo NP. They include: Noun (obligatory) and other optional elements: Adjective, Pronominal modifier, Numeral, Quantifier, Demonstrative and Relative Clause. He notes that the Noun is the only obligatory element within the NP, 'even though in (the surface form of) certain utterances, Pronouns, Numerals and interrogatives – the other nominals – may appear as the head of their NPs, only the N can really be called the Head of the NP'. Emenanjo (1978) does not make mention of determiner, but refer to the other constituents of the Igbo NP as 'nominal modifiers'. He defines nominal modifiers as 'those qualifying words which even though they only occur in the NP, can never be used alone in a minimal NP (p. 70). He mentions four nominal modifiers in Igbo: Adjective, Demonstrative, Quantifier and Pronominal Modifier.

Oluikpe (1979:23) probably influenced by the English determiners posits the Igbo determiner rule as follows:

(10)   Det———→ (Num) (Quant) (Part)(Gen)(Demon)

According to the rule, Igbo determiners consist of a string of such optional elements as Numeral (Num), Quantifier (Quant), Particularizer (Part), Genitive (Gen) and Demonstratives (Demon). This rule is supported by an NP such as 11.

(11)　　　akwụkwọ atọ　　niilē　　ṅkè　m　　ahụ̀
　　　　　N　　　　　Num　Quant　Part　Gen　Demon
　　　　　Book　　　　three　all　　　　　my　　those
　　　　　　　'all those three books of mine'

Oluikpe's (1978) view is that the elements in (11) (except the head N) are determiners.

The works mentioned above look at the noun phrase from the traditional view that a noun is the head of a nominal phrase. Mbah (2006) attempts to adopt the modern trend that determiner could have a phrasal projection DP. He however, implicitly rejects the DP-hypothesis as proposed in Abney (1987) by arguing that in Igbo, the noun is the head of the nominal phrase. He argues for the noun as the head from the semantico-syntactic notion of obligatoriness and a lexical element that could stand in place of the whole phrase. To him, the noun is the head while the modifiers are complements. He therefore proposes a different kind of DP different from Abney's proposal which 'unites all complements as a syntactic unit' (p.110). He defines a DP in Igbo as 'any category, whatever, which qualifiers, modifiers or quantifies a head so as to discriminate it from other hitherto identical lexical items'. Based on this definition, he gives the structure of a phrase such as (12a) as (12b).

(12)　　a.　　Ada ogologo ukwu ọcha anyi ...
　　　　　　　'Our light complexioned big tall Ada'

b.

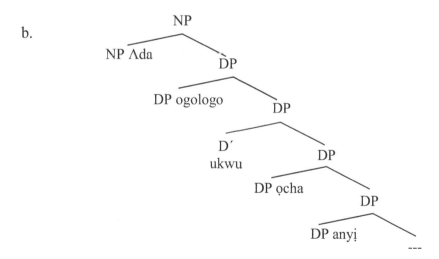

From the structure presented in (12b), there seems not be any syntactic unit that unites or dominates all the complements as he earlier claimed. Rather what we see in (12b) are different DPs being dominated by other DPs and the analysis does not suggest a recursive projection of the same category. There is no common head for the category D.

From the analysis presented in Mbah (2006), it is obvious that the idea behind the formulation of the DP-hypothesis is misconcieved. The DP hypothesis does not claim that the deteminer is the head of the Noun Phrase. The noun remains the head of the NP and N can take complements like adjectives and so on. What DP hypothesis claims is that the nominal phrase, in an argument position, has a functional element (seen or unseen) which gives the nominal phrase its features, like definiteness, genericity and specificity. This abstract node is called a D which is derived from the overt element traditionally designated as determiner. D takes NP as its complement. It has also been argued that within the nominal phrase, there could be other functional projections such as DemP and QP. However, the NP is the only obligatory phrase within the larger nominal phrase designated as DP.

We shall argue in chapter six, contrary to Mbah (2006), that Igbo has DP in the sense of Abney (1987).

3.4 Summary

In this chapter, we have examined previous works on Igbo functional categories. These categories have been described in Igbo by previous analysts. Majority of them used the descriptive method. Only very few gave these categories theoretical analysis. For example, Mbah (1999, 2006) uses the Government and Binding Framework to describe some of the Igbo functional categories especially the Infl categories. Dechaine (1993) also gives a lot of theoretical account of Igbo functional categories. From the review of these works, it is obvious that the present research has many areas of disagreement with the previous analyst, hence the justification for this research.

To the best of my knowledge, this represents the first major attempt to describe the Igbo functional categories in line with the current assumptions of the Minimalist Program outlined in Chomsky (1995) and subsequent works.

Chapter 4
Functional Categories in the Igbo Verbal Domain: A Description

4.0 Preliminaries

Some functional categories are predicate operators. They are closely associated with the verb. These categories include; tense, aspect, mood and negation. In this chapter, our focus is on these verbal functional categories; tense, aspect and negation and how they operate in Igbo.

We shall discuss the morphological realisations of these categories in Igbo. In the chapter that follows, we shall discuss them from the perspective the theoretical assumptions of the Minimalist program

Most of the illustrations are drawn from Standard Igbo but different dialectal variants are brought in when it becomes necessary for the purpose of comparison.

4.1 The Igbo Verb Root

Generally speaking, Igbo verb roots are monosyllabic with the form CV.

(1)   a.   ri   b.   gbu   c.   gwe
             'eat'   'kill'   'grind'

      d.   si   e.   gụ   f.   zà
             'cook'   'read'   'sweep'

There are few verb roots with more than one syllable structure[1] such as those in 2.

(2)   a.   kele   b.   gosi
             'greet'   'show'

Most times, the meaning of the verb root is not fully specified without the noun complement. This led to Emenanjo's (1975:41-42) generalisation that the 'Igbo verb obligatorily co-exists with a noun-the complement'. The intricate relationship between the verb and its complement, led to the classification of noun complements into object and inherent complements (cf. Nwachukwu 1985, Emenanjo 1975). The arguments for or against the classification is not within the purview of the present study. However, it should be noted that many verbs are meaningful only when cited with their complement.

---

[1] Some analysts (cf Uwalaka 1997) view 2 as cases of two bound roots. The parts are meaningless in isolation. This maintains the position that all Igbo verbs have the simple CV root.

For example, the verb *gba* may not be understood without the following NP complement as shown by 3.

(3)   a.   gba   bọọlụ̀
               V   ball
               'play or kick football'

        b.   gba   egwū
               V   dance
               'dance'

        c.   gba àmà
               V betrayal
               'betray'

        d.   gba egbè
               V   gun
               'shoot gun'

The verb stem can also be complex in any of the following ways. One, the verb stem could be as a result of compounding of two or more independent roots as in (4).

(4)   a.   gbu-dà
               cut-fall
               'cut down'

        b.   gba-bà
               run-enter
               'run into'

        c.   kụ̀-gbu
               hit-kill
               'beat to death'

Two, the verb stem could be a combination of a simple root and an extensional suffix as in (5).

(5)   a.   bù-te
               carry-towards
               'bring'

    b. chị – kọ
      pick – together
      'put together'

    c. rị – go
      climb – upward
      'climb up'

    d. kè – do
      tie – fast against
      'tie to'

Emenanjo (1978: 97) describes the extensional suffixes in (5) as 'meaning-modifiers, i.e. extending the meaning of the word with which they are used. Extensional suffixes may be used to show some aspectual distinctions that are not inflectionally marked. For example in (6) below, the suffixes are inceptive and iterative markers respectively.

(6)   a. rì – we
      eat – INCEP
      'begin to eat'

    b. mè – gide
      do – ITER
      'do repeatedly'

Emenanjo (1978) identifies about ninety extensional suffixes in Igbo. He does not claim that the list is exhaustive. There could be many more. Many of them are homophonous. We need to identify the extensional suffixes to be able to distinguish them from inflectional suffixes that mark tense, aspect and negation which are the focus of the present study.

  Some Igbo syntacticians classify Igbo verbs into tone classes. Nwachukwu (1995) and Uwalaka (1997) classify Igbo verb roots into three clauses: High, High-Low and Low. According to Uwalaka (1997:48),

> Igbo monosyllabic verbs can also be sub-divided with respect to tone. The Central dialect areas have three tone classes of verbs since they make a three way distinction, High, High-Low, and Low. However, other dialects, like Ọnịchà and Ọhụhụ, make a two way distinction. In these dialects, the High and High-Low verbs occur as High-Low.

The following table illustrates the three tone classes and their behaviour in different verb forms: infinitive, imperative and general subjunctive.

Table IV: Tonal classes of Igbo verbs

Tone Class	Verb root	Infinitive	Imperative	Subjunctive
Class 1 High	ri 'eat'	i-rī	ri-e	ri-e
	lụ 'marry'	ị-lụ̄	lụ-ọ	lụ-ọ
	gbu 'kill'	i-gbū	gbu-o	gbu-o
Class 2 High--Low	ga 'go'	ị-gā	gà-a	gà-a
	ti 'shout'	i-tī	tì-e	tì-e
	me 'do'	i-mē	mè-e	mè-e
Class 3 Low	zà 'sweep'	i-zà	zà-a	zà-a
	chè 'think'	i-chè	chè-e	chè-e
	mụ̀ 'learn'	ị-mụ̀	mụ̀-ọ	mụ̀-ọ

Observe that while tone class 2 verbs share the same infinitive and subjunctive forms with tone class 1 (High), it shares the same imperative form with tone class 3 (Low).

The importance of understanding the tonal classes of Igbo verbs in Igbo syntax cannot be overemphasized. This is because, according to Nwachukwu (1995:14), 'The verb is the only lexical class in Igbo that undergoes inflection. Inflection produces a number of verb-forms which express specific time (tense or aspect) meanings'. These inflectional affixes cause tonal changes which are predictable depending on the inherent tone of the verb root. This is why it is important to classify Igbo verbs along tonal lines.

4.2 Igbo Auxiliary Verbs

Auxiliary belongs to the closed class. In other words, their number is limited. Emenanjo (1985) carried out an extensive work on Igbo auxiliaries. He did an extensive review of previous analyses of Igbo auxiliaries. The summary of his review is that the number of auxiliaries in Igbo is dependent on the dialects under focus and the approach adopted by the analyst. It may not be possible to capture all the arguments on the number and syntactic behaviour of auxiliaries in Igbo, but what one can say here is that Emenanjo observes that two auxiliaries *ga* and *na* are common in most dialects of Igbo. However, he identifies some others which are dialect-specific in different Igbo lects. Following the structuralist approach, Emenanjo (1985:50) characterises the Igbo auxiliaries as follows.

i)   Auxiliaries are helping verbs which obligatorily require some nomino-verbal complement.

ii) In some dialects, especially the Ọnicha group, the nomino-verbal is always a participle, i.e. E + verb root. In the Central dialects, it is either a participle or an infinitive, i.e. I + verb root.

iii) Auxiliaries combine with main verbs to produce subtle and significant changes in meaning.

iv) While some auxiliaries in some dialects can take inflections, some do not.

Inasmuch as auxiliary is not the major focus of this work, we would like to comment on point number (ii) above which says that the nomino-verbal complement of the auxiliary can be a participle in some dialects but can occur as a participle or infinitive in some other dialects. The participle verb form is the form of the verb that takes a harmonising prefix e/a. This prefix is seen as nominalising because it gives the verb the characteristics of a noun. Evidence that the nomino-verbal element (participle) behaves like a noun is from its inability to assign Accusative Case to the following noun complement. However, Dechaine (1993:472) observes that the participle assigns Genitive Case to the following noun. This could be seen with H or H-H nouns. According to her, a logical object surfaces as H-H when in the Accusative Case in factative (7a & 8a), but surfaces as H$^!$H when in the Genitive Case after a participle (as in future and durative constructions in (7b) and (8b) respectively). The NPs in question are underlined.

(7)   a.   Òbi rì-rì   <u>nri</u>
             Obi   eat-FACT food
             'Obi ate food'

        b.   Òbi gà è-ri   <u>nrī</u>
             Obi   FUT e-eat food
             'Obi will eat food'

(8)   a.   Ada bè-rè   <u>akwa</u>
             Ada   cry-FACT cry
             'Ada cried'

        b.   Ada nà   è-be   <u>akwā</u>
             Ada   DUR e-cry cry
             'Ada is crying'

This same downstepping of high could be seen in associative constructions where the second NP is assigned inherent Genitive Case.

(9)　　　a.　isi + aka　———▶　　isi akā
　　　　　　　head hand　　　　　　'thumb'

　　　　　b.　ome + ji　———▶　　ome jī
　　　　　　　tendril yam　　　　　　'yam tendril'

　　　　　c.　ụlọ̀ + ewu　———▶　　ụlọ̀ ewū
　　　　　　　house goat　　　　　　'goatshed'

Dechaine (1993:473) following Manfredi (1991) concludes that all the noun-internal downsteps are realisations of inherent (Genitive) Case. According to her, 'This means that whenever an aux is present, the main verb does not assign its usual structural (Accusative) Case. The unavailability of structural Case is related to the presence of the toneless e- prefix on the main verb'. We shall in this study gloss the harmonic nominalising *e-/-a* prefix as 'e' wherever it occurs in our data.

We now return to the issue of whether the auxiliary verb can take as complement the participle form discussed above as well as take the infinitive form in the Central dialects as claimed. In the Central dialects, (10a & b) are obtainable.

(10)　　　a.　Òbi　　gà　　è-ri　　nrī
　　　　　　　Obi　　AUX　*e*-eat food
　　　　　　　'Obi will eat food'

　　　　　b.　Òbi　　gà　　i-rī　　nrī
　　　　　　　Obi　　go　　INF-eat food
　　　　　　　'Obi is going to eat'

We do not agree that *ga* in (10b) is an auxiliary verb as most analysts claim (including Emenanjo 1985). Emenanjo himself notes on page 53 that,

> All analysts seem to be unanimous in giving a lexical meaning of something that has to do with 'going to' to this auxiliary. This unanimity derives partly from the fact that this auxiliary is clearly either the same as or is related to the verb-ga 'go' 'pass' in the eyes of the different analysts, and partly also because one uses 'go to' to express the future in English. Thus with a lexical meaning of 'going to' 'ga is used to mark a notion which has been called 'future' or 'futurity' in Igbo.

Emenanjo's statement above suggests that *ga* as an auxiliary verb probably derived from the verb *ga* 'go'. What we are contending is that auxiliaries do not allow infinitival verb forms as complements in the Central dialects as claimed. We would rather view *ga* in (10b) as a main verb translatable to 'going' in English. We see (10b) as a sequence of two verbs within a monoclausal structure where the first verb *ga* takes the infinitive *iri nri* as its complement. If auxiliaries can take infinitive verb form as complement, then nothing stops the other auxiliaries in the Central dialects from taking the same infinitive complement. But this is not the case as exemplified by the unacceptability of (11b) and (12b).

(11)   a. Ọ nà è-ri ji
       3S AUX(DUR) *e*-eat yam
       'S/He is eating yam'

     b *Ọ nà i-rī ji
       3S AUX(DUR) INF-eat yam

(12)   a. O jì à-ṅụ oke mmị̀ị̀ (Owere dialect)
       3S AUX(HAB) *e*-drink much wine
       'S/He drinks too much wine'

     b. * O jì i-ṅū oke mmị̀ị̀
       3S AUX(HAB) INF-drink much wine

Our position is that *ga* in (10a) is an auxiliary verb. But it can still be used as lexical main verb 'going' to express future. Emenanjo himself observed that "one uses 'go to' to express the future in English". Since other clearly established auxiliaries do not allow infinitive forms as complements, we conclude that *ga* as an auxiliary does not take infinitive complement, but *ga* as a verb does.

  Igbo auxiliaries (and auxiliaries in general) are functional elements. What is not clear is whether they should be seen as functional projections, AUXP or morphosyntaxtic spell-out of other functional heads: Tense, Aspect, Mood and Negation.

  Following Carnie (2007:217), we assume in this study that the auxiliary verb is generated inside the VP in layers, where the auxiliary verb takes another VP containing the main verb as its complement. This is contrary to the older assumption that auxiliary verbs are generated in addition to the categories of tense and aspect under a separate node called Aux (cf. Chomsky 1965). The auxiliary verb inside the VP layer is demonstrated in (13) (adapted from Carnie, 2007:217).

(13)

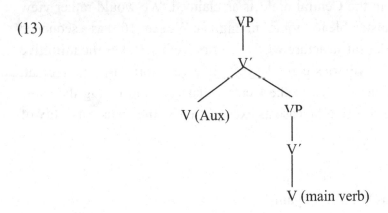

When an auxiliary verb is present in Igbo, it can bear the inflectional affixes normally associated with the main verb. This imples that the auxiliary verb can take overt or zero affixes to mark different grammatical categories such as tense, aspect and negation. When an auxiliary verb is present, it is the auxiliary that undergoes v-movement to check features, while the main verb remains in-situ (See section 5.1 for detailed discussion of v-movement and feature-checking).

Apart from the two common auxiliaries in Igbo discussed above, there are others which could be found in different dialects of Igbo. Emenanjo (1985) identifies more auxiliaries in the dialects he studied. They are shown in table V below.

Table V: Some auxiliary verbs from different Igbo dialects

Aux	Function	Dialect(s)	Example of use
ga	Future (anticipative)	Standard Igbo & most dialects	Ọ gà àgụ akwụkwọ 'He will read'
na/la	Durative	Standard Igbo & most dialects	Ọ nà èri nrī 'He is eating'
ji	Durative (Habitual)	Owere and some Central dialects	O jì ànụ oke mmìì 'He drinks a hot'
ya	Future (anticipative)	Nneewi	Ọ yà àbia 'He will come'
ha	Durative negative	Nneewi	Ọ ha èli nnī He does not eat
ma	Future negative	Ọnịcha	Ọ ma eli ifē 'He will not eat'
te	Past	Igbouzo and most Niger West dialects	Ada tè mà mmā 'Ada was beautiful'
ka	Unfulfilled	Standard Igbo and most dialects	Ọ kà abia ebe à "He should have come here'

The table shows that auxiliary verbs could be used to mark tense, aspect and polarity distinctions. Some of the auxiliaries such as *ga* and *na* take inflectional affixes. For example *ga* and *na* take the general negative suffix *ghị*.

(14)   a.   Òbi nà à-zụ ahịa akwà
                Obi DUR e-sell market cloth
                'Obi sells clothes'

         b.   Òbi a-nā-ghī   à-zụ ahịa akwà
                Obi Agr-DUR-NEG e-sell market cloth
                'Obi does not sell clothes'

(15)   a.   Ike gà   à-ga Aba
                Ike FUT *e*-go Aba
                'Ike will go to Aba'

         b.   Ike a-gā-ghị̄   a-ga Aba
                Ike Agr-FUT-NEG *e*-go Aba
                'Ike will not go to Aba'

         c.   Ọ̀ ga-ghị̄   a-ga Aba
                3S FUT-NEG *e*-go Aba
                'S/He will not go to Aba'

Some of the auxiliaries are used only in the negative such as Nneewi *ha* and Ọnịcha *ma*

(16)   Òbi a-hā   à-zụ afịa akwà   (Nneewi)
         Obi Agr-DUR.NEG e-sell market clothes
         'Obi does not trade in clothes'

(17)   Ike a-mā   e-je Aba   (Ọnịcha)
         Ike Agr-FUT-NEG e-go Aba
         'Ike will not go to Aba'

It is important to note that tone plays an important role especially in the dialects with suffixless negative constructions. We shall return to the role of tone in Igbo negation in section 4.3.3 where negation will be discussed.

4.3 Igbo Verbal Inflectional Categories: A Description

Three types of grammatical categories are marked inflectionally on the Igbo verb. They are tense, aspect and negation. We shall take up these categories one after the other.

4.3.1 *Tense in Igbo*

Tense is the grammaticalization of time in relation to the utterance. The use of the term 'grammaticalization' implies morphological marking. In this sense, traditional grammarians refer to languages that do not have tense morphemes as 'tenseless' (cf. Lyons 1968). The assumption of Universal Grammar is that tense is a universal category irrespective of whether it is morphological marked in the language or not. In the GB framework, tense is assumed to be an obligatory feature of every finite clause. Infl is said to have the features [+ TNS + AGR]. Following the UG assumption on the universality of tense, let us examine how the three basic tense distinctions are marked in Igbo, starting with the past tense.

4.3.1.1 *Past Tense*

We have noted that the rV factative can co-occur with an rV past, at least in some dialects. It seems that in most dialects, factativity and tense are marked by only one rV suffix. In this case, the interpretation of the verb as either present or past is dependent on the semantic features of the verb. If the verb is [+ eventive], the rV suffix is given a past tense reading.

(18)   a.   Òbi gbù-rù   agwọ
                 Obi kill-FACT.PAST snake
                 'Obi killed a snake'

           b.   Ibè rụ̀-rụ̀   ụlọ̀
                 Ibe build-FACT.PAST house
                 'Ibe built a house'

           c.   Àmadi zù-rù   ohi   jī
                 Amadi steal-FACT.PAST stealing yam
                 'Amadi stole yam'

           d.   Ha gbà-rà   m̀gba
                 3P wrestle-FACT.PAST wrestling
                 'They wrestled'

           e.   O sì-rì   ofe egusi
                 3S cook-FACT.PAST soup melon
                 'S/He cooked melon soup'

If, however, the verb has the feature [- eventive], then the rV suffix lacks a past tense reading as shown by (19).

(19)   a.   Àda   nwè-rè   egō
             Ada   own-FACT money
             'Ada has money'

         b.   Ụlùmmā   mà-rà   mmā
             Ụlụmma   be beautiful-FACT beauty
             'Ụlụmma is beautiful'

In a simple indicative sentence, the verb root and the rV suffix have L-L tone pattern, irrespective of the tone class of the verb root.

In the 'Inland West Igbo dialect cluster' (Ikekeonwu 1987), the rV suffix is realized as *lụ, lị* or *lV*. The examples below are from Nneewi dialect.

(20)   a.   Òjukwū   gbà-lụ̀   bọọlụ̀
             Ojukwu   play-FACT.PAST ball
              'Ojukwu played football'

         b.   O gbù-lù   òke
             3S kill-FACT.PAST rat
              'S/He killed a rat'

         c.   Mèzie   gò-lù   motò   ọfụụ̄
             Mezie   buy-FACT.PAST car   new
             'Mezie bought a new car'

In most of the 'Niger Igbo dialects' (Ikekeonwu 1987) such as Igbouzo, Issele-Uku and Ika, the rV suffix is dropped entirely. Consider the examples below from Issele-Uku dialect.

(21)   a.   Awelē   lì   nni
             Awele   eat.FACT.PAST food
             'Awele ate food'

         b.   Fụṁnanya gbà   ṁgba   ṅnyàa
             Fụmnanya wrestle.FACT.PAST wrestling yesterday
             'Fụmnanya wrestled yesterday'

         c.   O gbù   mmadụ̀
             3S kill.FACT.PAST person
              'S/He killed somebody'

One piece of evidence supporting the fact that the rV suffix is dropped in the West Niger dialects is the identical tone pattern seen in most of the dialects of Igbo. The verb root and the suffix are always on L – L tone pattern. In the dialects, where the suffix is dropped, the verb root retains the low tone. Compare (22) below with (21c) above.

(22)   Oò   gbu   mmadụ̀
              3S.DUR kill person
              'S/He kills'
              'S/He is a killer'

(22) is a durative aspectual construction. The verb root in (22) bears a high tone unlike in the past tense construction in (21c). The structures have almost identical segmental morphological make-up, except for the elongation of the vowel of the third person subject pronoun. This lengthening is required to bear the low tone of the dropped durative auxiliary *nà*, present in Standard Igbo and most dialects of Igbo, as shown in (23).

(23)   Ọ nà   è-gbu mmadụ̀
              3S AUX(DUR) e-kill person
              'S/He kills OR S/He is a killer'

When the subject is a lexical NP, the *e*-prefix on the verb bears the low tone as shown in (24).

(24)   Àmaka è-gbu   mmadụ̀
              Amaka DUR-kill person
              'Amaka is a killer'

Observe that the verb *gbu* in (22), (23) and (24) bears high tone unlike in (21c) where it bears low tone. We therefore associate the low tone on the verbs in (21) to the underlying presence of the rV factative/past suffix which is always on a low tone in simple indicative sentences.[2]

The evident dropping of the rV suffix and the durative auxiliary in the Niger Igbo dialects as demonstrated by (21), (22) and (24), points to one thing. The Niger Igbo dialects rely more on tonal melody to mark grammatical contrasts. The segmental

---

[2]The verb form with rV suffix is usually on L-L tone pattern except in structures like relative constructions where the H-H tone pattern is the indicator of subject relativisation. Compare a& b

   a.   nwokē gbù-rù mmadụ̀   b.   nwokē gbu-ru mmadụ̀ ...
        man   killed person   man   killed person
        'A man killed somebody'   'The man who killed somebody ...'

morphemes are elided at the surface, but their tones remain as the overt reflexes of their underlying existence.

Emenanjo (1985) subsumes the discussion of past under aspect. He does not recognise tense as a category in Igbo, but observes on page 80, that "past is marked by... rV (past) in Ezinaihite and Ọhụhụ among the Central dialects". He identifies other past markers in different dialects of Igbo: *-bụ* suffix in Nneewi, *-naana* suffix in Owere and *te* auxiliary in Igbouzo. We shall demonstrate that the rV suffix (with its dialectal variants: lụ, lị, etc) is a past tense marker while these other forms are 'base-generated V^0 time adjuncts' (Dechaine, 1993:474). We shall use Nneewi *-bụ* to illustrate the point. Examine the data below from Nneewi.

(25)   a.   Emeka zụ̀-bụ̀-lụ̀   afịa   n' Ọnịcha
              Emeka sell-PRIOR-FACT.PAST market at Ọnịcha
              'Emeka used to be a trader at Ọnicha'

      b.   Ike gbà-bụ̀-lụ̀   bọọlụ
              Ike   play-PRIOR-FACT.PAST ball
              'Ike used to play football'

      c.   Ngọzị mà-bụ̀-lụ̀   mmā
              Ngọzị be.beautiful-PRIOR-FACT beauty
              'Ngọzị used to be beautiful'

      d.   Ike kpụ̀-bụ̀   atụrụ̄
              Ike pull-PRIOR sheep
              'Ike was pulling a sheep'

(25a&b) are eventive verbs, while (25c&d) are stative verbs. (25d), even though it is semantically eventive, it is used here to refer to a state of carrying just like the verbs of wearing. While (25c) seems to have a past meaning because of the presence of *-bụ* suffix, compared to its absence in (26) below:

(26)   Ngọzị mà-lụ̀   mmā
          Ngozi be.beautiful-FACT beauty
          'Ngozi is beautiful'

It is actually a time adjunct which has attached to the verb in surface syntax. Certain classes of stative verbs do not take the rV suffix. Some of them from Emenanjo (1985: 176) are listed below.

i   *The copulas*   bụ̀ 'be' (+ general identification)
                         dị̀ 'be' (+ quality or property)

ii   *Locative verbs* e.g.

                    dị̀ 'be –at'
                    nọ̀ 'be – at'
                    bì   'reside at'

iii   *Verbs describing carrying* e.g.

                    kpà   'hold in the hand'
                    bù   'carry on the head'
                    kwọ̀ 'carry on the back'

The verb *kpụ̀* in (25d) belongs to the class of verbs describing carrying and therefore, does not require the *lụ* suffix. In the absence of a suffix, such verbs are always interpreted as present.

(27)   Ike kpụ̀ atụrụ̄
              Ike   pull sheep
              'Ike is pulling a sheep'

The presence of *bụ* therefore gives (25c & d) their past tense reading. But, is *bụ* actually a grammatical past tense marker? Consider (28) – (31).

(28)   a.   Emeka zụ̀-lụ̀   afịa   n' Ọ̀nìchà
                 Emeka sell-FACT.PAST market at Onicha
                 'Emeka was a trader at Onicha'

        b.   Emeka zụ̀-lụ̀   afịa   n' Ọ̀nịchà (nà) m̀bụ
                 Emeka sell-FACT.PAST market at Onicha at   first
                 'Emeka traded at Onicha previously'
                      OR
                 'Emeka used to be a trader at Onicha'

(29)   a.   Ike gbà-lụ̀   bọọlụ̀
                 Ike play-FACT.PAST ball
                 'Ike played football'

b.   Ike gbà-lụ̀   bọọlụ̀ (nà) m̀bụ
  Ike play-FACT.PAST ball   at   first
  'Ike played football previously
     OR
  'Ike used to be a footballer'

(30)   Ngozi mà-lụ̀   mmā (nà) mbụ
     Ngozi be.beautiful-FACT beauty at   first
     'Ngozi used to be beautiful before'

(31)   Ike kpụ̀ atụrụ̄ (nà) mbụ
     Ike pull sheep   at   first
     'Ike was previously pulling a sheep'

(28) – (31) have past reading without the *bụ* suffix. (25a) and (28b) have the same interpretation, likewise (25b) and (29b). Onukawa (1994:25) observes that the -bụ suffix as in (25) is "a reflex of the noun m̀bụ 'first, before, formerly'". He mentions that Emenanjo (1979) and Williamson (1972) share the same view with him. In line with Onukawa's view, we argue that the time adjunct *mbụ* which is the complement of an elided preposition gets attached to the verb as a suffix *–bụ* just like other inflectional suffixes. It seems that *mbụ* grammaticalised and became an inflectional suffix marking the aspect 'Priorness' (Dechaine 1993). The *lụ* factative morpheme remains the indicator of past tense in (28) and (29). In (30), the *lụ* suffix does not encode past tense, likewise the bare form *kpụ* in (31). The only indicator of past in (30) and (31) is the past time adjunct *mbụ*.

The suffix *bụ* seems to carry with it the notion of a state that has ceased to exist. Compare the pairs of examples in (32) and (33).

(32)   a.   Òbi gbù-lù   mmadụ̀
      Obi kill-FACT.PAST person
      'Obi killed somebody'

    b.   Òbi gbù-bụ̀-lụ̀   mmadụ̀
      Obi kill-PRIOR-FACT.PAST person
      'Obi used to kill or Obi was a murderer'

(33)   a.   Nneka sì-lù   nni
      Nneka cook-FACT.PAST food
      'Nneka cooked'

b.   Nneka sì-bụ̀-lụ̀   nni
        Nneka cook-PRIOR-FACT.PAST food
        'Nneka used to cook or Nneka was a cook/caterer'

(32) and (33) show that an active verb which would normally take a *lụ* suffix to mark simple past, can take, in addition, a *bụ* suffix to show a state that is no longer existing. That is why (32b) for instance could be interpreted as 'Obi was a murderer' and not 'Obi murdered or killed somebody'. In a situation where the verb does not depict any state, then the expression with *bụ* suffix (34b) is a direct paraphrase of the expression with *mbụ* time adjunction (34c).

(34)   a.   Ike gò-lụ̀   motò
                Ike buy-FACT.PAST car
                'Ike bought a car'

        b.   Ike gò-bụ̀-lụ̀   motò
                Ike buy-PRIOR-FACT.PAST car
                'Ike bought a car previously'

        c.   Ike gò-lụ̀   motò (nà) m̀bụ
                Ike buy-FACT.PAST car   at   first
                'Ike bought a car previuosly'

Our data therefore support the assumption that *bụ* is a time adjunct which has incorporated on the verb. In Nneewi, the *bụ* suffix does not harmonise with the vowel of the verb as shown in 34 above. It is important to note that Dechaine's (1993) claim that *bụ* does not attach directly to the auxiliary is wrong. She rules out (35b) as unacceptable.

(35)   a.   Ànyị̀ nà   è-li-bụ̀   nnī
                1P   AUX(DUR) e-eat-PRIOR food
                'We used to eat'

        b.   Ànyị̀ nà-bụ̀   è-li nnī
                1P   AUX(DUR)-PRIOR e-eat food
                'We used to eat'

(35b) is judged acceptable by most native speakers of Nneewi. (36b & c) below also support the fact that *bụ* can attach to the auxiliary verb.

(36)   a.   Ọ   ha   è-li-bụ   nnī
              3S   AUX(DUR.NEG)   e-eat-PRIOR   food
              'S/He was not eating before now'

         b.   Ọ   ha-bụ   è-li   nnī
              3S   AUX(DUR.NEG)-PRIOR   e-eat   food
              'She was not eating before now'

         c.   Ọ   ha-bụ   è-li-bụ   nnī
              3S   AUX(DUR.NEG)-PRIOR   e-eat-PRIOR   food
              'She was not eating before now'

It is also possible to find *bụ* attached to both the auxiliary and the main verb as in (36c) above. It is interesting to note that the three structures in 36 have exactly the same meaning. This implies that the time adjunct has the option of attaching to either the main verb or the auxiliary or both. We propose (37) as the derivational structure of the –*bụ* suffix (The specifier positions are omitted).

(37)

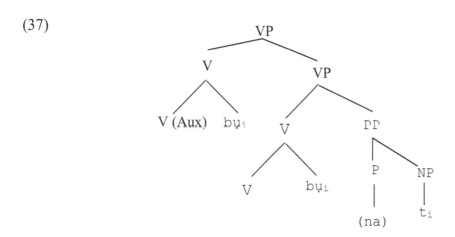

(37) shows that the NP complement of the PP adjunct of the VP, *mbụ* can move and adjoin to either the main verb or the Aux or both as a suffix *bụ*. The structure in (37) is contentious, owing to the fact that a moved item should not have overt spell-out in two locations. However, it is acceptable within the theory that a moved item could land in some other positions before its final position, leaving behind intermediate traces. We therefore do not see any reason why the trace of a moved item cannot have an overt spell-out just like the resumptive pronoun attested in the literature. This means that the adjunct in (37) moves first to V before moving to Aux. The adjunct can optionally be spelt-out in any of the positions.

4.3.1.2 Present Tense

Present tense seems not to be distinctively marked in Igbo. Uwalaka (1988:53) observes that Igbo does not have one particular verb form for expressing present meaning. Some verbs could appear bare. This is the group of stative verbs listed by Emenanjo (1985:176). In their bare forms, they express present meaning.

(38)   a.   Àmaka wụ̀ nwokē
                  Amaka be man
                  'Amaka is a man'

          b.   Uzè   bì n'elu osisi
                  squirrel live on top tree
                  'A squirrel lives on a tree'

          c.   Ike kpù   òkpu mmeē
                  Ike wear cap   red
                  'Ike is putting on a red cap'

          d.   Nnekà kpụ̀ atụrụ̄
                  Nneka pull sheep
                  'Nneka is dragging a sheep'

          e.   Ọ nọ̀ n'elu ube
                  35 be on top pear
                  'He is on top of a pear tree'

          f.   Ùju bù   ìtè mmīrī n'isi
                  Uju carry pot water on head
                  'Uju is carrying a water pot on her head'

Some of the stative verbs allow the rV suffix and still maintain a present reading.

(39)   a.   Àda mà-rà   mmā
                  Ada be.beautiful-FACT beauty
                  'Ada is beautiful'

          b.   Ike bù-rù   ibù
                  Ike be.fat-FACT fatness
                  'Ike is fat'

c.   Nnekà nwè-rè   ụlọ̀
        Nneka own-FACT house
        'Nneka owns a house'

Most eventive verbs will express present meaning, using *na* auxiliary durative aspect marker, which could be given either a habitual reading or a progressive reading in most dialects.

(40)   a.   Òbi nà è-ri edè
                Obi DUR e-eat cocoyam
                'Obi eats cocoyam'   (Habitual reading)
                 OR
                'Obi is eating cocoyam'   (Progressive reading)

        b.   Àmàlà   nà   à-gba àkwụ̀nàkwụ̀nà
                Amala   DUR e-run prostitution
                'Amala is a prostitute'   (Habitual reading only)

It seems that no particular morpheme marks present tense in Igbo. In this respect, the present tense in Igbo is similar to the present tense in English which is also phonologically null. The third person singular agreement morpheme '-s' is the only morphological indicator of the present tense in English.

(41)   a.   He kills birds

        b.   They kill birds

In the absence of the agreement morpheme, the present verb form is bare as in (41b).

        If we assume tense to be a semantic notion that is interpretable at LF, we therefore posit a zero morpheme for present tense in Igbo.

4.3.1.3 Future Tense

In the literature, future time is sometimes treated as tense, sometimes as aspect and sometimes as mood, depending on the language. Emenanjo (1985) treats future as aspect in Igbo. He refers to it as the 'anticipative aspect'. This is because he belongs to the school of thought that does not recognise the category of tense in Igbo. He admits that there are 'few instances of tense' in Igbo. According to him,

> Aspect is more prominent than tense as a category in Igbo. For ease of reference, therefore, we shall treat the few instances of tense under aspect. We shall also,

because of the predominance of aspect, treat 'future' as an aspect in this study. But instead of future aspect, we shall following Whorf (1938) call it ANTICIPATIVE (ANT) since it indicates that an action is anticipated, i.e. it has not yet started but its start is expected or anticipated (Emenanjo 1985:21)

Future tense is not marked by a verbal affix in Igbo but rather by an auxiliary verb *gà*. This seems to cut across all the Igbo dialects. The auxiliay *gà* has different dialectal variants, for example, *yà* in Nneewi and *jà* in Orumba.

The future auxiliary takes a verb as complement and the verb appears in its participial form (i.e. e + verb root) examples are shown below.

(42)   a.   Òbi gà   à-gba ọsọ̄
                  Obi FUT e-run running
                  'Obi will run'

          b.   Ha gà   à-zụ uwe ọhụụ̄
                  3P FUT   e-buy cloth new
                  'They will buy new clothes'

          c.   Ndi ezè gà   è-nwe nzùkọ
                  Pl. king FUT e-have meeting
                  'Kings will have a meeting'

          d.   Ibè gà   à-bụ onye   isī
                  Ibe FUT e-be person head
                  'Ibe will be the leader'

The auxiliary verb *ga* is always on a low tone irrespective of the inherent tone of the main verb. Since future is marked by an auxiliary verb and Igbo auxiliaries are aspectual in nature, we follow Emenanjo (1985) to assume that future is aspectually marked in Igbo. We turn now to aspect.

4.3.2 *Aspect in Igbo*
Aspect, no doubt, is more clearly marked in Igbo than tense. This is because apart from the rV past tense marker which also marks factative aspect, all other tenses are either marked by zero affix or implied in aspectually marked constructions. There are several aspectual distinctions which combine in some intricate ways with the other inflectional categories: tense, and negation. Emenanjo (1985:20) observes that aspect in Igbo is marked both inflectionally and derivational through:

i.   extensional suffixes such as

   - we   inceptive
   - riri   continuative
   - dide   iterative
   - kwasi   repetitive
   - lari   pluperfective

ii.   Inflectional suffixes such as

   = lE, = nE, =go   perfective
   = ghE, ga   progressive

iii.   auxiliary verbs or aspectual markers such as

   na   durative, progressive, habitual
   ga   anticipative

Our focus is on (ii) and (iii) above which are instance of inflectional marking of aspect.

In the literature on aspect (cf. Comrie 1976, Dahl 1985, Bhat 1999), two basic distinctions are normally made: perfective and imperfective. Accordingly to Comrie (1976: 16), 'Perfectivity indicates the view of a situation as a single whole, without distinction of the various separate phases that make up that situation, while the imperfective pays essential attention to the internal structure of the situation'. Perfectivity implies a completed process, while imperfectivity views a process as on-going. Imperfectivity can be further subdivided. Aspectual distinctions such as progressive, iterative, habitual, etc, are assumed to be subdivisions of imperfective.

We shall discuss the perfective, the progressive and the habitual which are inflectionally marked in Igbo.

4.3.2.1 Perfective Aspect

Perfectivity is marked in Standard Igbo by the *-la* suffix. There are many dialectal variants of this suffix: *-nE, -lE, -go,- ge, -gwo, -gwee, -gwele, -wo,* etc. In Standard Igbo, the perfective verb form has the following morphemic structure.

(43)   E + CV + A + La
             Where E = a/e harmonic prefix, CV = verb root,
             A = Open Vowel Suffix (OVS) and La = perfective suffix

The structure in (43) is exemplified in (44).

(44)   a.   Ibè à-zụ-ọ-la   akwà ọhụrụ
                 Ibe AGR-buy-OVS-PF cloth new
                 'Ibe has bought a new cloth'

b.   Àmaka e-gbu-o-la   ekē
        Amaka AGR-kill-OVS-PF python
        'Amaka has killed a python'

The question is whether perfectivity is jointly marked by the prefix, the open vowel suffix and the -*la* suffix as claimed by some Igbo linguists? (cf. Emenanjo 1978, Green and Igwe 1963). Our answer is in   the negative. The -*la* suffix is the only morphosyntactic spell-out of the perfective aspect in Standard Igbo. What then is the function of *e-* prefix and the open vowel suffix?

The *e-* prefix does not occur in all instances of perfective construction. Consider:

(45)   a.   O gbū-o-la   ekē
                  3S kill-OVS-PF python
                  'S/He has killed a python'

          b.   Ị zū-ọ-la   àlà
                  2S buy-OVS-PF land
                  'You have bought land'

          c.   M gā-a-la   Aba
                  1S go-OVS-PF Aba
                  'I have gone to Aba'

          d.   A-gā-a-la   m Aba
                  Pref-go-OVS-PF 1S Aba
                  'I have gone to Aba'

Sentences 45(a-c) have clitic pronouns in the subject positions. Anyanwu (2005), Eze (1995) and Obiamalu (2010) have argued that the pronominal clitic pronouns are functional heads occupying the AGR head position. This agreement element encodes the phi-features of the subject DP. This analysis implies that Igbo could be a quasi pro-drop language. Negative construction also instantiates the agreement pattern.

(46)   a.   Ha e-gbū-ghi   eke
                  3P AGR-kill-NEG python
                  'They did not kill a python'

          b.   Ò gbu-ghi   eke
                  3S kill-NEG python
                  'S/He did not kill a python.

Why this kind of agreement pattern is seen only in the negative and perfective constructions will be discussed in chapter 5 (section 5.1.3). We gloss this *e-* prefix as AGR. Observe that in (45c&d), the first person singular pronoun subject can optionally come after the verb. The third person plural subject pronoun also behaves this way as shown in (47).

(47)   a.   Ha a-ga-a-la   Aba
                 3P AGR-go-OVS-PF Aba
                 'They have gone to Aba

           b.   A-ga-a-la   hà Aba
                 AGR-go-OVS-PF 3P Aba
                 'They have gone to Aba.

It is not clear why only the first person singular and the third person plural behave this way. What they have in common is that they are the only subject pronouns that begin with a consonant. Others begin with a vowel. The post verbal subject pronoun in (45d) and (47b) seems to give support to the VP-Internal subject Hypothesis. The verb moves out of the VP to the higher functional heads. The subject pronoun remains in-situ in the Spec VP giving rise to the order, VSO. In the absence of a subject in the Spec AGR position, the *e-* prefix agreement element occurs as the 'subject' of the sentence. We shall return to the status of *e-* prefix in chapter five (section 5.1.3)

The open vowel suffix (OVS) in Igbo, occurs in a variety of constructions: imperative, perfective, conditional and subjunctive. Our view, is that, the OVS is an empty morpheme, in the sense that it lacks semantic content. It serves as a stem extender. We base our argument on three pieces of evidence.

One, the OVS does not occur in perfective constructions where the verb root has a CVV syllable structure as in (48).

(48)   Ọ bịa-la
              3S come-PF
              'He has come'

Two, the OVS does not occur where the verb root is a complex one (a verb with more than one root) as shown is (49).

(49)   a.   Ike e-gbū-dà-la   nkwū   ahụ̀
                 Ike AGR-cut-fall-PF palm tree that
                 'Ike has cut down that palm tree'

b. Ọ zụ-ta-la   ụgbọ àlà ọhụrụ
 3S buy-Ext.suff.-PF vehicle land new
 'S/He has bought a new car'

Three, in dialects where the perfective is marked by the suffix -*go* and other phonologically related variants: -*gwo, -wo, -gwe,* the OVS does not occur. Consider (50) from Ọnịcha dialect.

(50) a. O gbū-gō ekē
      3S kill-PF python
      'S/He has killed a python'

    b. O gō-gō ụnọ̀ n' Ọ̀nịchà
      3S buy-PF house at Onicha
      'S/He has bought a house at Onicha'

    c. Taàgbo e-je-go afị̄a
      Taagbo AGR-go-PF market
      'Taagbo has gone to the market'

The fact that the OVS can occur in a variety of constructions in Igbo, coupled with the fact that it does not occur in all instances of perfective constructions in Igbo, points to the fact that the OVS is an empty morpheme. It is a stem extender. Our position is supported by the work, Eme and Mbagwu (2009), which analyses the Igbo OVS as a connective

4.3.2.2 Durative Aspect

Durative aspect expresses an action that is taking place or on-going at a particular point in time. It could be an on-going process at the time of speaking, traditionally referred to as present continuous. It could be an on-going process at a point in time in the past, traditionally referred to as past continuous. It could also refer to a habit which has been going on over a period of time, either in the present or in the past. The present and past continuous are usually referred to as progressive aspect while a habitual action is referred to as habitual aspect.

   Progressive and habitual are subdivisions of imperfective since an imperfective process or state is typically stable through time. Emenanjo (1985) uses the term 'durative' as a cover term for progressive and habitual, since most dialects of Igbo do not distinguish the two. In some Central dialects e.g. Owere, 'there is a systematic syntactic distinction between progressiveness and habituality' (Emenanjo 1985: 122).

We shall discuss the distinction in the Owere dialect, but first, let us examine how durative aspect is marked in Standard Igbo.

The durative aspect is usually marked by the auxiliary *na*.

(51) a. Ike nà   è-ri ji
          Ike DUR e-eat yam
          'Ike is eating yam'   (Progressive reading)
          'Ike eats yam'   (Habitual reading)

      b. Ọ nà   à-gụ akwụkwọ
          3S DUR e-read book
          'S/He is reading a book'   (Progressive reading)
          'S/He reads OR S/He is a student' (Habitual reading)

      c. Àmàlà   nà   a-zà   ụlọ̀
          Amala   DUR e-sweep house
          'Amala is sweeping the house'   (Progressive reading)
          'Amala sweeps the house'   (Habitual reading)

      d. Ọ nà e-chè   echìchè
          3S DUR e-think thought
          'S/He is thinking'   (Progressive reading)
          'S/He thinks'   (Habitual reading)

The durative auxiliary *na* always bears a low tone and takes a nomino-verbal as complement. The nominalising prefix *e-* verbal prefix bears a low tone if the verb root is a High Tone Verb (HTV) as in (51a & b). The same prefix bears a high tone, if the verb root is a Low Tone Verb (LTV) as in (51c & d). We shall discuss the implications of these tonal alternations for v-movement in chapter five (section 5.2.2). We turn now to durative aspect in Owere.

4.3.2.2.1 Progressive in the Owere dialect

In Owere, the durative aspect could be divided into progressive and habitual. Progressive is marked by a non-harmonising inflectional suffix *-ga*. The examples are adopted from Emenanjo (1985: 122) (glossing is mine)

(52)   a. O rĭ-ga   rĭ   à
                3S eat-PROG food Dem
                'S/He is eating this food'

b.   Àdha   mā-ga   mmā
      Ada   be.beautiful-PROG beauty
      'Ada is becoming beautiful'

c.   Ànyi   kwù-gà   ụkhà
      1P   speak-PROG talk
      'We are talking'

d.   Àdha   zà-gà   ụyọ̀
      Ada   sweep-PROG house
      'Ada is sweeping the house'

e.   Nwatā   à   vù-gà   ivù
      child   Dem be.fat-PROG fatness
      'This child is becoming fat'

The data show that the *-ga* suffix bears high tone with HTVs, but bears low tone with HLTVs and LTVs.

4.3.2.2.2 Habitual in the Owere dialect

Unlike many other Igbo dialects, the habitual is distinctively marked from the progressive. The syntactic structures are different. The habitual in Owere is marked by an auxiliary *ji*, and just like every other auxiliary in the language is complemented by the nomino-verbal. Unlike the other auxiliaries, *ji* does not accept any affix. It bears a low tone. The examples below are also drawn from Emenanjo (1985:123).

(53)   a.   O jì   a-zà   ụyọ   à
                3S HAB e-sweep house Dem
                'S/He usually sweeps this house'

          b.   Àdha   jì   è-kwu ụkhà
                Ada   HAB e-talk   talk
                'Ada is a talkative'

          c.   Àdha   jì   è-je ǹga nwo
                Ada   HAB e-go place 3P
                'Ada usually goes to their place'

The habitual constructions in Owere have the same syntactic and tone patterns with the durative *na* in Standard Igbo.

4.3.3 Negation in Igbo

Negation is usually seen as a subcategory of the category known as polarity. Polarity bifurcates into affirmation and negation. In the description of polarity, negation is usually the main focus since in most languages, only negation is marked and the absence of negative markers implies affirmation. Lyons (1977) defines negation as a "denial of an assertive proposition or a predictation that a proposition is untrue".

Different languages employ different methods of marking negation. Dahl (1979) typified different languages based on their negation marking strategies. Some of the strategies include; the use of negative particles, affixation, independent lexical item, prosodic melody (tone and intonation). Igbo employs two strategies: affixation and tonal melody. There is no independent negative marker in Igbo and negation without the verb is impossible in Igbo. This is unlike English, Yoruba and Hausa that have negative particles. Negation in Igbo is affixal in nature. It is dependent on the verb. Igbo has no independent negative particle. This could explain why constituent negation of nouns is possible in English, Hausa and Yoruba but not possible in Igbo

(54)   a.   No   money   (English)
                NEG noun

        b.   Kòsí ówó   (Yoruba)
                NEG money
                'No money'

        c.   Baa kudi   (Hausa)
                NEG money
                'No money'

        d.   *Ego-ghi   (Igbo)
                  money NEG

        e.   Egō   a-dị̄-ghī   (Igbo)
                Money Agr-V-NEG
                'No money'

54d is impossible because the negative suffix cannot be used to directly negate a noun. This could explain why constituent negation of an NP must involve a cleft construction where the NP is moved to a focal point as the subject or object of a semantically dummy verbs: *nwe, bụ* or *dị* which bear the negative suffix. This is shown in 60c.

(55)   a.   Obi zù-rù   ụlọ̀   (affirmative)
                Obi buy-rVpast house
                'Obi bought a house'

b.   Obi a-zū-ghị   ụlọ̀   (sentence negation)
        Obi AGR-buy-NEG house
        'Obi did not buy a house'

c.   Ò nwe-ghi ụlọ̀   Òbi zụ̀-rụ̀   (constituent negation)
        It be-NEG house Obi buy-rV(past)
        'Obi bought no house'

The general negative marker in Igbo is the suffix *-ghi*. The negative suffix can attach to all types of verbs; main verb, auxiliary, stative, non-stative. The negative verb form has the following morphemic structure

(56)   E + CV + ghi

                where E = e/a harmonizing prefix, CV = verb root,
                ghi = negative suffix

Examples of affirmative sentences and their negative counterparts are shown in table III below (different verb types are represented)

Table VI: Affirmative and negative verb forms

S/N	Affirmative	Negative
1	Àda mà-rà mmā Ada be.beautiful-rV beauty 'Ada is beautiful'	Àda a-mā-ghi mmā Ada AGR-be.beautiful-NEG beauty 'Ada is not beautiful'
2	Ọ zụ̀-rụ̀ akwà 3S buy-rV(past) cloth 'S/He bought some clothes'	Ọ zụ-ghị akwà 3S buy-NEG cloth 'S/He did not buy any cloth'
3	Ike nà à-gba egwū Ike DUR e-dance dance 'Ike is dancing'	Ike a-nā-ghi à-gba egwū Ike AGR-DUR-NEG e-dance dance 'Ike is not dancing'
4	Ị̀ gà è-si jī echi 2S FUT e-cook yam tomorrow You will look your tomorrow	Ị̀ ga-ghị̄ è-si jī echi 2S FUT-NEG e-cook yam tomorrow You will not cook yam tomorrow

Observe that when the subject DP is a clitic pronoun, the *e-* prefix does not occur in the negative. We have earlier noted that the same pattern occurs in the perfective construction. We have been glossing this prefix as Agr and we shall demonstrate in chapter five (section 5.1.3), that the prefix is not part of a discontinuous negative morpheme contrary to the general belief in Igbo linguistics.

4.3.3.1 Negative Perfective Form

The negative perfective has a more complex structure. It is marked by *-beghi*, which seems to be a combination of two morphemes: *be*, negative suppletive form of the perfective marker and *ghi*, general negative marker. Dechaine (1993:470) sees *-be* as a negative polarity item, translatable to 'yet' in English. 'Yet' is an NPI which semantically implies imperfective, i.e. non-completive it naturally occurs in the negative form of perfective constructions in English, exemplified in (57b).

(57)   a.   He has done it

          b.   He has not done it yet

(58) and (59) below are examples of perfective constructions in the affirmative and in the negative.

(58)   a.   Òbi e-ri-e-la   nrī
              Obi AGR-eat-OVS-PF food
              'Obi has eaten'

          b.   Òbi e-ri-bè-ghì   nri
              Obi AGR-eat-PF-NEG food
              'Obi has not eaten'

(59)   a.   Ọ bịa-la
              3S come-PF
              'S/He has come'

          b.   Ọ̀ bịa-bè-ghị̀
              3S come-PF-NEG
              'S/He has not come'

We have said that *–be* is a suppletive form of the perfective marker that occurs only in the negative. It could occur without the negative suffix *ghi* as shown in (60) below.

(60)   a.   Òbi e-ri-bè-è   nri
              Obi AGR-eat-PF-NEG food
              'Obi has not eaten'

          b.   Ọ bịa-bè-è
              3S come-PF-NEG
              'S/He has not come'

The elision of the general negative marker *ghi* necessitated the lengthening of the vowel of the negative perfective element. Observe that *-be* and *-ghi*[3] are on low tone in (58b) and (59b). The extra syllable in (60) also bears low tone. It seems that the extra syllable is there to bear the low tone of the elided *-ghi* suffix. The elision of the negative suffix is one of the features of language where economy is a desideratum, in line with the MP principles.

4.3.3.2 Negative Imperative Verb Form

The negative imperative form is marked by the suffix *-la*. It is sometimes referred to as the prohibitive. The *-la* prohibitive suffix is homophonous with *-la* that marks perfective. The negative imperative verb form has the following morphemic structure.

(61)   E + CV + la

Where E = e/a prefix, CV = verb root, la = imperative negative suffix

Here are some examples.

(62)   a.   Rì-e   nri ahù
               eat-OVS food Dem
               'Eat that food'

          b.   E-rī-la   nri ahù
               AGR-eat-PROH food Dem
               'Do not eat that food'

(63)   a.   Zà-a   ụlọ̀
               sweep-OVS house
               'Sweep the house'

          b.   A-zà-là   ụlọ̀
               AGR-sweep-PROH house
               'Do not sweep the house'

(64)   a.   (Ụnụ̀) gbà-a   ọsọ̄
               2P   run-OVS run
               'You (pl.) should run'

---

[3] ghi is inherently toneless, its tone is determined by the tone of the preceding syllable. It takes low after low tone preceding syllable or downstep after high tone preceding syllable.
E.gs Ò righī, Ọ̀ zaghì, Ò ribèghì

    b.   (Ụnụ̀) a-gba-la   ọsọ
        2P   AGR-run-PROH run
        'You (pl.) should not run'

Naturally, commands are only given to the addressee (second person). When the subject is the second person singular, it is left unexpressed. But, when it is the second person plural there are two options in the imperative. The second person plural pronoun can occur in the subject position before the verb as in (64) or as an enclitic after the verb as in (65) below.

(65)   a.   Gbà-a-nụ̀   ọsọ
                run-OVS-2Pencl. run
                '(You pl.) Run'

        b.   A-gba-la-nụ̀   ọsọ
                AGR-run-PROH-2Pencl. run
                '(You pl.) Do not run'

Notice that the OVS does not occur in the prohibitive which is another piece of evidence that the OVS is an empty morpheme as we have earlier claimed in this study. Observe also that the prohibitive has the Agr prefix as in the negative and the perfective constructions. What do they have in common? We shall answer this question in chapter five (5.1.1)

4.3.3.3 Negative Auxiliary Verbs

There are some Igbo lects such as Nnewi and Onicha where some auxiliary verbs are inherently negative in meaning. Compare the affirmative sentences and their negative counterparts in Nneewi and Onicha below.

(66)   (Nneewi)
        a.   Ọ nà   è-li   nnī
                3S DUR e-eat food
                'S/He is eating'

        b.   Ọ̀ ha   è-li   nnī
                3S DUR.NEG e-eat food
                'S/He is not eating food'

        c.   Èmeka nà à-gụ akwụkwọ
                Emeka DUR e-read book
                'Emeka is reading'

d.   Ėmeka a-hā   à-gụ akwụkwọ
      Emeka AGR-DUR.NEG e-read book
      'Emeka is reading'

(67) (Ọnicha)

      a.   Ọ gà a-zà   ụnọ̀
            3S FUT e-sweep house
            'S/He will sweep the house'

      b.   Ọ ma   n-zà   ụnọ̀
            3S FUT.NEG e-sweep house
            'S/He will not sweep the house'

      c.   Ngọzị gà a-la   mmīlī
            Ngọzị FUT e-drink water
            'Ngozi will drink water'

      d.   Ngọzị a-mā   n-la   mmīlī
            Ngọzị AGR-FUT.NEG e-drink water
            'Ngozi will not drink water'

In Nneewi, the durative auxiliary *na* has a negative counterpart *ha*. While in Onicha, the Future (anticipative) auxiliary *ga* has *ma* as its negative counterpart. Observe that in Onicha, the nomino-verbal complement of the auxiliary verb takes *n-* prefix in the negative.

      The role of tone in the negative construction cannot be ignored. It is very obvious in dialects where negative auxiliaries exist. For example, in Nneewi dialect, there is no way of distinguishing (68a & b) below except by tone.

(68) a.   Ọ yà è-li nnī
            3S FUT e-eat food
            'S/He will eat food'

      b.   Ọ̀ ya   e-li nnī
            3S FUT.NEG e-eat food
            'S/He will not eat'

(68) presents some interesting insight into the role of tone in Igbo negation. Ndimele (1995, 2004, 2009) claims that a floating low tone plays important role in Igbo negation. According to him, 'The low tone on the subject pronominal clitics in negative constructions is due to the presence of an abstract (underlying) floating low tone. What

happens is that the underlying floating low tone merely displaces the high tone feature of the subject pronominal clitic' (Ndimele 2009:133). Is it actually the low tone of the subject clitic pronoun or the high tone of the auxiliary verb *ya* that marks negation in (68b)? Now consider, in addition these two other possible tone patterns for the same structure.

(69) a. Ọ̀ yà è-li nnī
        3S FUT e-eat food
        'Will s/he eat food?'

     b. Ọ yā   e-li nnī
         3S FUT.NEG e-eat food
         'Will s/he not eat'

Our focus here is on the tone pattern of the two elements: subject pronoun and the following auxiliary. The tone of the verb root and its prefix follows from the tone of the auxiliary preceding them. Let us show the tone patterns observed in 68 and 69 and their meanings in table VII below.

Table VII: Tone patterns in Nneewi affirmative/negative-interrogative constructions

Data Nọ	Tone on the subject pronoun	Tone on the auxiliary verb	Meaning
68a	H	L	Future affirmative
68b	L	H	Future negative
69a	L	L	Future affirmative interrogative
69b	H	S	Future negative interrogative

From the table, one can easily see at a glance that the auxiliary is constantly on low tone in the affirmative and on high tone in the negative. In the negative interrogative, the auxiliary bears a step tone which is caused by the underlying low tone interrogative marker which forces the high tone negative marker to become a step tone. The subject pronoun has no tone pattern that correlates with any of the meanings. The pronoun bears low tone in the affirmative in (69a) but high tone in (68a). It bears high tone in the negative in (69b) but low tone in (68b). The same pronoun bears low tone in the interrogative in (69a) but high tone in (69b). From this analysis, it is clear that the tone on the subject pronoun is not the indicator of negation, but rather the tone on the auxiliary verb. This suggests that Ndimele's assumption that low tone plays an important role in Igbo negation might not be correct. It is rather the high tone that plays an important role in Igbo negation. We shall show in chapter five (5.2.2), the role of high tone in Igbo negation.

4.5 Summary

In this chapter, we have have described the morphological realizations of the functional categories found within the Igbo verbal domain. We looked at tense, aspect and negation. Our analysis reveals that only the past tense is morphologically marked in Igbo. Other tenses: present and future are not marked. The durative aspect encodes present tense while the anticipative aspect encodes future tense.

Chapter 5
Functional Categories in the Igbo Verbal Domain: A Theoretical Analysis

5.0   Preliminaries

In this chapter, we shall apply the theoretical issues raised in chapter two in the analysis of the functional categories discussed in the immediate preceding chapter. We start immediately with the discussion of v-movement and feature-checking and go on to relate these theoretical assumptions to Igbo functional categories in the verbal domain.

5.1   Igbo Functional Categories, V-movement and Feature-checking

In Chapter Four, we have been looking at the morphosyntactic spell-out of the verbal functional categories in Igbo. In this section, which is more theoretically oriented, we shall look at how the verb moves to check its features against the features of the associated functional categories: T(ense) Asp(ect) and Neg(ation). We shall also look at the structural relationships between the verb and the associated functional categories.

One of the Minimalist assumption is that lexical categories (verbs, nouns, adjectives, adverbs) are fully inflected in the lexicon. That is, that all the affixes are attached to the lexical item before any movement takes place. According to Marantz (1995: 366),

Vs and Ns are taken from the lexicon fully inflected with inflectional affixes. The inflectional nodes in the syntax are not associated with affixes (nor with any phonological content whatsoever) but simply with certain features: Tense, Case and Agreement features among others. Nevertheless, specific bundles of these features of the category AGR and T are lexical items. This is a radical deviation from the earlier assumption within the older models of TGG (Standard theory to GB) that affixes move to get attached to the lexical categories, especially the verb. This was referred to as the Affix-hopping transformation (cf. Chomsky 1965, Akmajian and Heny 1975, Bach 1974, among others)

Igbo inflectional categories are realised as verbal affixes or as auxiliaries. It is assumed that the verb with its affixes moves from within the VP and adjoins to the relevant functional heads: T, ASP and NEG to check its features against the features of the functional heads. For example, a verb with tense affixes will move to T to check its tense features. It is important to note that sometimes, the affixes may not be overt, but the Conceptual-Intentional aspect of the grammar (i.e. Logical Form) leads us to posit null affixes which have to be checked by the relevant functional heads.

Feature checking is simply the elimination of uninterpretable features (i.e features that play no role in semantic interpretation). Only the interpretable features (i.e.

features that play roles in semantic interpretation) eventually reach the C-I interface level (i.e. LF in the earlier framework).[1]

V-movement is assumed for Igbo because the Igbo verb bears all kinds of affixes marking different grammatical categories. Igbo verbs rarely occur in their bare forms both in finite and infinitival clauses. Dechaine (1993: 456) observes that amongst the Kwa languages, Igbo has exceptionally rich inflectional morphology. The rich inflection of the Igbo verb triggers off v-movement. According to Dechaine, the major difference between Igbo and Yoruba (a typical analytic Kwa language) is the presence of v-movement in the former and its absence in the latter.

In the sub-sections that follow, we shall discuss v-movement as it relates to the functional heads: T, ASP and NEG in Igbo.

5.1.1 *V-movement and T*

The universality of tense as a grammatical category is one of the major assumptions of the UG based syntactic theories. Dechaine (1993:17) states this in form of a hypothesis which she refers to as the 'TP-hypothesis'. The hypothesis says that 'all matrix predicates have a Tense projection. Even if tense does not have morphological content, it is still present as a syntactic position'. Within the GB framework, it is assumed to be present in every finite clause as one of the features of the INFL head. The other feature being Agreement. In the Minimalist framework, following from Pollocks (1989), Tense is assumed to be the head of a separate functional projection: TP. We have earlier noted, that within MP, tense morphemes are assumed to be part of the verb in the lexicon, thus dropping the earlier assumption that tense lowers to be attached to the verb. In this sense, word-formation, i.e. merging elements that make-up words, is removed from the domain of syntax (Benmamoun 2000: 13). The implication of this new assumption is that verbs with tense affixes have to move to the abstract T head, where the tense features are checked.

We have mentioned in chapter four (4.3.1) that most Igbo linguists do not accept that tense is morphologically marked in Igbo. Also supporting the view that Igbo has no tense morpheme are Dechaine (1993) and Manfredi (1991). Dechaine (1993) analyses the so called past aspect markers of Emenanjo (1985) as 'priorness aspect' marker and maintains that Igbo has no tense morpheme.

Uwalaka (1988, 2003) tends to disagree with the 'popular' view that Igbo has no tense morpheme. According to Uwalaka (2003:3), 'We need... to establish that Igbo, contra to Emenanjo (1976) and Manfredi (1991) has a morphosyntactic realisation of the category, Tense". To her, the rV verbal suffix is a past tense marker. She provides the following sentences as illustrations of the use of rV suffix to mark past tense.

---

[1] We have discussed features and feature-checking in the first chapter. For a more detailed and simplified discussion of feature checking, see Radford 1997, 2004.

(1)   a.   Òbi gbù-rù   agwọ
                Obi kill-rV(past) snake
                'Obi killed a snake'

        b.   Àda gà-rà   ahịa
                Ada go-rV(past) market
                'Ada went to the market'

        c.   Ụlùmmā kù-rù   nwa n' Àba
                Ụlụmma carry-rV(past) child at Aba
                'Ụlụmma was a baby nurse at Aba'

        d.   Ogù gbu-dà-rà   osisi
                Ogu cut-fell-rV(past) tree
                'Ogu cut down a tree'

        e.   Ùju   gà-à-rà   i-kwū   okwu
                Uju   AUX-rV(past)-rV(pluperf.) INF-talk talk
                'Uju would have talked'

        f.   Òbi bì-rì   Mbọsị
                Obi live-rV(past) Mbosi
                'Obi lived at Mbosi

                              (Adapted from Uwalaka 2003:4)

The examples in (1) represent active verb (1a-d), stative verb (1f) auxiliary verbs (1e) and complex predicate (1d). In all instances, the rV suffix indicates past. Without the suffix, (1c & f), for example, will have present tense reading as shown in (2).

(2)   a.   Ụlùmmā kù   nwa
                Ụlụmma carry baby
                'Ụlụmma is carrying a baby'

        b.   Òbi bì Mbọsị
                Obi live Mbosi
                'Obi lives at Mbosi'

It is not as if those who claim that there is no tense morpheme in Igbo were not aware of such examples as cited by Uwalaka, but they argue that the rV suffix marks factative rather than tense. (cf. Welmers and Welmers 1968, Emenanjo 1985, Dechaine 1993,

Manfredi, 1991) Their argument is based on the fact that the same rV suffix can occur with certain verbs especially stative verbs where no past tense reading is implied as in (3).

(3)   a.   Ada ma-ra   mma
              Ada be.beautiful-rV beauty
              'Ada is beautiful'

       b.   Uche to-ro   Ogologo
              Uche be.tall-rV tallness
              'Uche is tall'

Is the rV suffix in (3), the same as the rV suffix in (1)?[2] I would adopt the position of Uwalaka in arguing that the rV (past) is different from the rV (factative). In fact, in Ezinaihite Mbaise dialect, the two can co-occur as shown in (4).

(4)   a.   Àda mà-à-rà   mmā m̀gbè ọ bụ̀ nwatà
              Ada be.beautiful-rV(Past)-rV(Fact.) beauty when 3S be child
              'Ada was beautiful when she was a child'

       b.   O bù-ù-rù   ibù
              3S be.fat-rV(Past)-rV(Fact.) fatness
              'S/He used to be fat'

Our glossing in (4) shows that we do not dispute the fact that the rV suffix marks factativity, but rather, we argue that tense and factativity could be marked by one and the same rV suffix in most dialects. The fact that the factative rV occurs only in finite clauses and never with infinitivals suggests that factativity is associated with finiteness and finite clause are [+Tense]. The rV suffix could therefore be seen as a cumulative exponent of factativity and tense. Tense could have the value [+ Past] in active verbs and [+ Present] in stative verbs. The rV suffix in (1a) and (3a) could be glossed as in (5a) and (5b) respectively.

(5)   a.   Òbi gbù-rù   agwọ
              Obi kill-FACT.PAST snake
              'Obi killed a snake'

---

[2] Different types of rV suffixes have been identified in Igbo. See especially Green and Igwe (1963: 54-55), Winston (1973: 153-154), Nwachukwu (1977: 114-143) Uwalaka (1988:52-54) and Ọnụkawa (1994)

b. À̀da mà-rà   mmā
    Ada be.beautiful-FACT.PRES beauty
    'Ada is beautiful'

We have argued in section 4.3.1.1 that past tense could be supported by time adjunct which can undergo head movement and get incorporated on the verb. This is exemplified by *bụ* in Nneewi. The examples below are illustrative.

(6)   a.   Ike gò-lụ̀   motò̧
             Ike buy-FACT.PAST car
             'Ike bought a car'

       b.   Ike gò-bụ̀-lụ̀   motò
             Ike buy-PRIOR-FACT.PAST car
             'Ike bought a car before now'

       c.   Ike gò-lụ̀   motò (nà) m̀bụ
             Ike buy-FACT.PAST car   at first
             'Ike bought a car before now'

Onukawa (1994), Emenanjo (1979) and Williamson (1992) have observed that –*bụ* suffix in (6b) is a reflex of, or probably derived from the noun *mbụ* 'first' in (6c).

Having established that past is marked by the rV suffix in Igbo, what can we say about the other tense features: present and future? We have shown in chapter four (section 4.3.1.2) that present tense has no overt morphological form. Present tense is indicated if the verb appears bare or if the rV suffix marks only factativity. Most times, present tense is implied in the durative aspect. Future is marked by the auxiliary verb *ga*. The future auxiliary *ga* seems to be aspectual i.e. 'Anticipative aspect' (Emenanjo 1985). This is because all the other auxiliaries in Igbo mark aspect. However, future tense is implied when aspect is anticipative.

Given our analysis above, it then means that Tense and Aspect exist as grammatical categories in Igbo. The verb moves first to Aspect and them to Tense. If there is no tense morpheme, the verb moves to Aspect and does not move further to Tense. This analysis is based on the assumption that only verbs with overt morphemes need to move overtly to the relevant functional heads to check the features associated with those morphemes. If there is no overt morpheme, the verb will only undergo covert movement at LF. In such case, where there is no tense morpheme, T has a zero realisation. Remember that factativity belongs to Aspect and that we have argued that an rV suffix can cumulatively mark factative aspect and past tense. If that is the case, a verb with the rV suffix will move to ASP and then to T to check its tense and aspectual features. (5a) for example, will then have the following structure.[3]

(7)

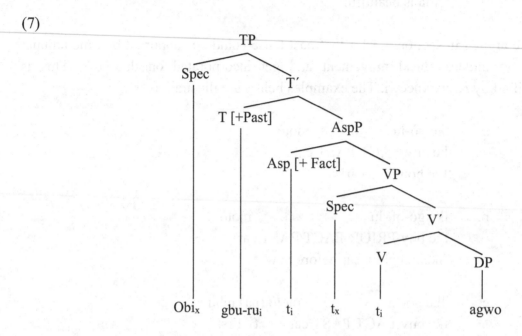

(7) shows that the verb *gburu* moves first to ASP to check its factative aspectual feature and then to T to check its past tense feature. (5b) will have the structure in (8).

(8)

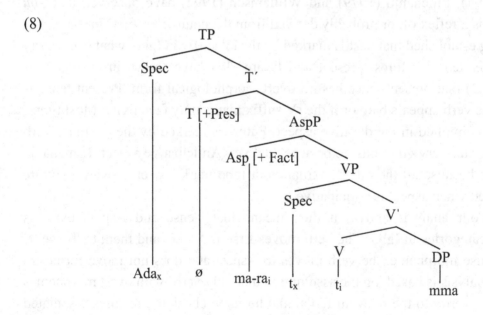

---

[3] The tree diagrams are simplified leaving out the AgrP nodes and pretending for now that the subject DP occupies the Spec TP position. Other irrelevant Spec nodes are also omitted.

While (4a) will have the structure in (9) below.

(9)

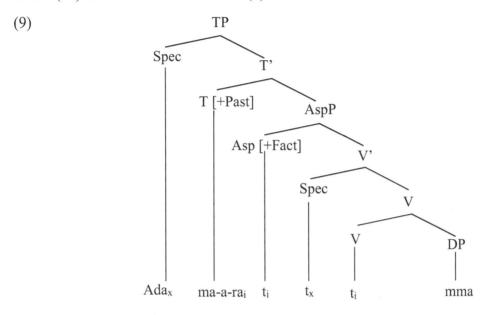

(8) shows that the verb moves to Asp to check its factative aspectual feature, but does not move further to T because present feature of T has no overt morphemic realization. It rather undergoes LF movement to T to check its present tense feature. T has zero realisation in (8). (9) shows that the verb moves to Asp and then to T because both aspectual and tense morphemes are present. (6b), from Nneewi, has a more complex structure as shown in (10) below.

(10)

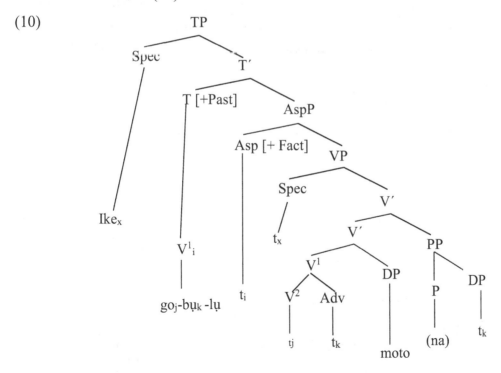

The complexity in (10) is as a result of the adjunction of the DP complement of the preposition to the verb.[4] The complex verb form, *go-bu* bearing the inflectional suffix *–lu* that marks factativity and tense, moves first to Asp and them to T. V[1] is used here to represent the complex verb. While V[2] is the simple verb root.

Having discussed factativity as aspect, let us now look at the other aspectual features as they relate to v-movement in the following section.

5.1.3   V-movement and ASP

We have earlier observed that majority of the linguists who have worked on Igbo are agreed that aspect is more clearly marked in Igbo than tense. We have also argued in the immediate preceding section that Asp as well as T is a functional head in the Igbo clause. This is because, in most cases, there is one aspectual feature or the other associated with the sentence. Even our rV past has factative aspectual feature associated with it.

Aspect could be marked suffixally, as well as with auxiliary verbs. We shall look at the perfective aspect which is marked by suffixation and the durative and anticipative aspects which are marked by auxiliary verbs. We shall then relate them to v-movement.

The perfective aspect is marked by the *-la* suffix which has many dialectal variants. We have shown in section 4.3.2.1, that the other morphemes associated with the perfective verb form: *e-* prefix and OVS perform different functions other than marking perfectivity. (See section 4.3.2.1 for details of the argument)

The perfective verb form moves to ASP to check its features. The T node which has the value (+Past) in Igbo perfective constructions remains empty because no tense morpheme is attached to the verb. (11a) below will have the structure in (11b).[5]

(11)   a.   Ọ   zụ-ọ-la   ụlọ̀
             3S   buy-OVS-PF house
             'S/He has bought a house'

---

[4] Alternatively, we can assume that this adjunction (attachment) takes place in the lexicon since word-building within MP is assumed to occur before entering the domain of syntax.

[5] We have so far assumed that subjects occupy the Spec position of TP when in actual fact, they occupy the Spec of AGR. But the analysis in (11b) presents a problem for this adhoc assumption, since clitic pronouns do not actually occupy the Spec position but rather base-generated in the AGR head position. We shall show this in 5.1.2. The analysis in (11b) is therefore wrong but we use it here for expository purposes, since we have not yet introduced the AGR node in our analysis

(11)   b.

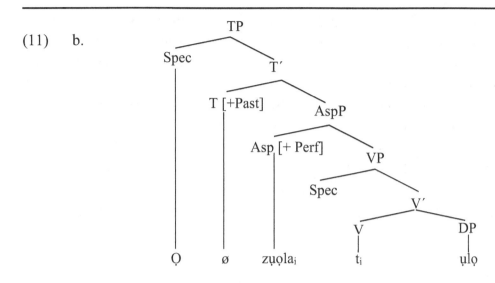

(11b) shows the verb moves to Asp but does not move further to T. The verb undergoes covert movement to T at LF to check its past tense feature.

The durative aspect is marked by an auxiliary verb *na* in Igbo. This implies that auxiliary verbs do move, just like the main verbs. A simple durative aspectual construction such as (12a) will be represented as in (12b).

(12)   a.   Òbi   nà   a-kụ̀   azụ̀
            Obi   DUR   e-fish   fish
            'Obi is fishing'

       b.

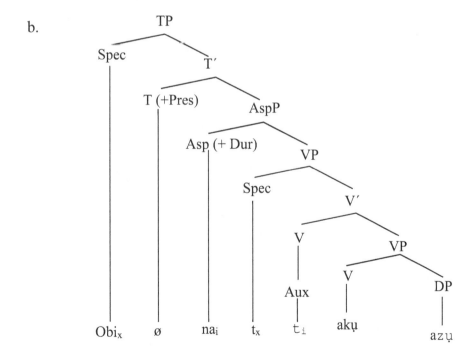

(12b) shows that the auxiliary verb is generated within the VP in layers (cf. Carnie 2007: 217, Dechaine 1993: 147). The auxiliary *na* moves to ASP, while the main verb *a-kụ* remains in-situ. Dechaine (1993) has argued that the presence of the nominalising prefix on the verb is an evidence that it does not undergo v-movement. Emenanjo (1985) refers to the verb form as nomino-verbal. This is the form traditionally referred to as participle. We have also argued in section 4.3 that the verb which is now nominal in charater does not assign structural Accussative Case to the DP complement. Rather the DP complement has inherent Genitive Case.

What obtains in the durative also obtains in the anticipative. The anticipative aspect is marked by the auxiliary *ga* and in such cases, T has the feature (+ Future). This is shown in (13) below.

(13)   a.   Òbi gà e-rī   jī
                Obi ANT e-eat yam

b.

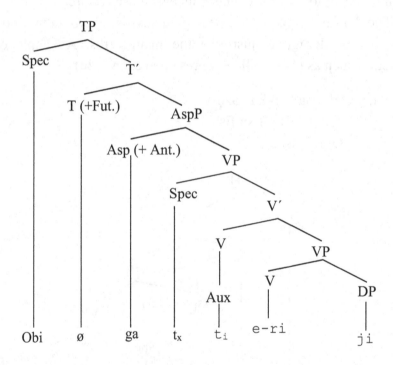

The alternative analysis will be to assume that T and ASP occupy the same position as proposed in Uwalaka (2003). We shall show why this proposal is not tenable when we look at v-movement and NEG in 5.1.3 below.

5.1.3 V-movement and NEG

Every human language possesses some formal ways of expressing negation. Löbner (2002:61) notes, 'it is no surprise then that all language have systematic means of the polar contrary of a sentence'. While the conveyed meaning and functions of negation are relatively uniform, the formal devices employed exhibit a considerable degree of variation across languages. Kitagawa (1986), Kayne (1989) and Pollock (1989) argue for the existence of a functional category NEG in Japanese, Romance languages and English respectively. While it is common knowledge that every language can express negation, it is not yet established whether negation exist as a functional head in every language (cf. Zanuttini, 1996). Dechaine (1993:135) notes, 'negation inhabits a borderline between functional and lexical projection. In Igbo, Neg has the status of a functional head, interacting with other functional heads T and ASP in X°-movement and feature-checking relationship'. The relative order of Neg among the other functional and lexical heads is parameterized. Neg projects higher than Tense in some languages and lower in some others. Zanuttini (1986:182) argues that in both Romance languages and English, the presence of NegP implies the presence of TP, because, according to him, 'given a TP, the NegP will be generated to its left so as to satisfy the selectional requirements of its head'.

  We assume here that NegP occurs lower than TP and AspP in Igbo as shown in (14) below. We shall justify the proposed structure in section 5.3. We shall also show why the negative morpheme and the tense morpheme do not co-occur.

(14)

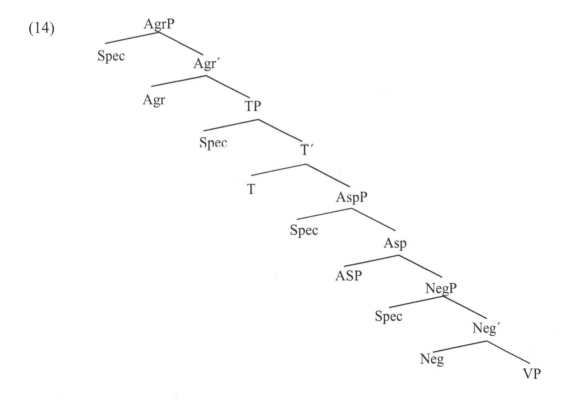

Since negation is morphologically marked in Igbo, it is assumed that v-movement to Neg occurs. Negation is marked in Standard Igbo by a suffix *ghi* which has no inherent tone. Interestingly, this suffix does not co-occur with the rV past and factative suffix as shown by (15)-(18).

(15) a.   Ezè rì-rì   nri
             Eze eat-FACT-PAST food
             'Eze ate food'

        b.   Ezè e-rī-ghī   nri
             Eze AGR-eat-NEG food
             'Eze did not eat food'

(16) a.   Ha mà-rà   mmā
             3P be.beautiful-FACT beauty
             'They are beautiful'

        b.   Ha a-mā-ghī   mmā
             3P AGR-be.beautiful-NEG beauty
             'They are not beautiful'

(17) a.   Ọ zà-rà   ụlọ
             3S sweep-FACT.PAST house
             'S/He swept the house'

        b.   Ọ za-ghì   ụlọ
             3S sweep-NEG house
             'S/He did not sweep the house'

(18) a.   E chè-rè   ṁ echìchè
             AGR think-FACT.PAST 1S thought
             'I had a thought'

        b.   È che-ghì   ṁ echìchè
             AGR think-NEG 1S thought
             'I did not think'

The data in (15)-(18) show that the rV suffix which marks tense and factativity is mutually exclusive with the negative marker. Even in the absence of the rV suffix, the negative sentences are given tense interpretation. It seems that the rV suffix does not occur in negative construction because negation is a denial of a fact and the rV suffix marks factativity. However, the same rV suffix also marks tense. In the absence of the rV suffix, how is tense marked in the negative construction? The answer is given in the next paragraph. Observe that in the negative construction, unlike in the affirmative, there is a harmonising prefix *e-/a-* which occurs if the subject DP is not a clitic. Clitic pronouns such as the third person singular, *o/ọ*, the second person singular, *i/ị*, the first person singular, *m* and the impersonal pronoun, *e/a* do not allow the *e-* verbal prefix. We have been glossing this prefix as 'AGR'.

We have presented in chapter four (4.3.3), the views of most Igbo analysts that negation in Igbo is templatic and comparable to French *ne ... pas* or the Hausa *ba ... ba* negation frame (cf. Emenanjo, 1985, Clark, 1989, Uwalaka, 2003, Ndimele, 2009). Dechaine (1993) does not agree with the template view of Igbo negation. She rather argues that the *e-* prefix in negative constructions is a 'default agreement' marker (Manfredi 1991) which surfaces as a result of stranded tense. According to Dechaine, 'Neg between T and V is a barrier for V to T movement. As V can't raise beyond Neg, T above Neg is empty'. The *e-* prefix surfaces in the Agr head position to give support to the empty T position which has strong tense features.

The presence of such *e-* prefix in Igbo perfective construction where no negation is implied, gives support to Dechaine's analysis and also supports our assumption that Tense and Aspect occupy different head positions, contrary to Uwalaka (2003). Consider (19) below.

(19)   a.   Àda a/à-zà-a-la   ụlọ̀
                Ada AGR-sweep-OVS-PF house
                'Ada has swept the house'

        b.   Ha a/à-zà-a-la   ụlọ̀
                3P AGR-sweep-OVS-PF house
                'They have swept the house'

        c.   Ọ zà-a-la   ụlọ̀
                3S sweep-OVS-PF house
                'He/She has swept the house'

        d.   Òbi è-gbu-o-la agū
                Obi AGR-kill-OVS-PF lion
                'Obi has killed a lion'

        e.   O gbu-o-la   agū
                3S kill-OVS-PF lion
                'S/He has killed a lion'

In the perfective construction the *e-* prefix occurs in exactly the same environment as in the negative construction. If the same kind of prefix will behave the same way in both negative and perfective constructions, then it cannot be part of a negative morpheme as claimed by Uwalaka (2003) Emenanjo (1985) and Clark (1989). However, if the *e*-prefix occurs as a result of Neg barrier as claimed by Dechaine (1993), how do we account for its occurrence in perfective constructions? Tense and aspect morphemes hardly co-occur in Igbo. The same with tense and negative morphemes. In the perfective aspect, tense morpheme is absent and so for that reason the verb does not raise to T. In other words, V moves to Asp and does not move further to T giving rise to the same *e*-prefix as support for strong tense feature that has no overt realisation.

We therefore modify Dechaine's Neg-barrier analysis by saying that in the absence of a tense affix, V does not need to move to T. But because the tense feature of T is strong in negative and perfective constructions, a default agreement element emerges to give support to the empty T head position. For example, a negative construction can be [+ past] without a past tense morpheme. The perfective construction has an implicit past tense reading.

Following our analysis, (15b) will have the structure in (20).

(15b)   Ezè e-rī-ghī   nri
                 Eze AGR-eat-NEG food
                 'Eze did not eat food'

(20)

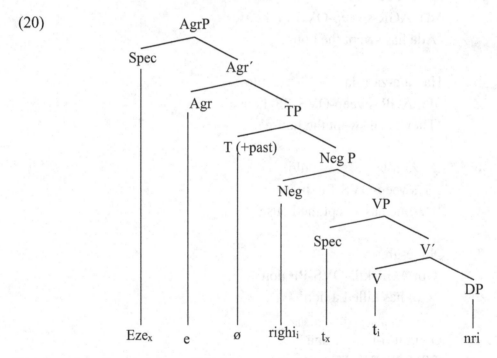

For the sake of comparison with the *e*- prefix in perfective construction, let us show the structure of the perfective construction in (19a) in (21).

(19a)   Àda à-zà-a-la   ụlọ̀
                   Ada   AGR-sweep-OVS-PF house
                   'Ada has swept the house'

(21)

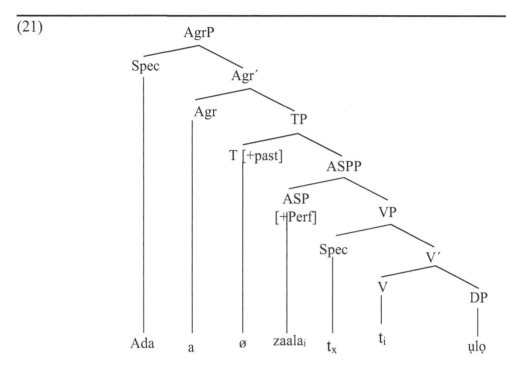

In (20), the verb raises to Neg and stops there. This leaves the T node empty. But because the T node has strong past tense feature, the agreement prefix gives morphological support to the otherwise stranded Tense. The same thing is applicable to (21), where the verb raises to Asp but does not raise further to T. T in (21) also has strong past tense feature. We therefore conclude that empty T head with strong tense features requires morphological support which comes in form of an agreement element.

It is important to note that this same Agr head position is where the clitic subject pronouns occur. (17b), for example (repeated here for convinence) will have the structure in (22).

(17b) Ọ̀ za-ghì ụlọ̀
       3S sweep-NEG house
       'S/He did not sweep the house'

Eze (1995), Anyanwu (2005) and Obiamalu (2010) have given some syntactic evidence in support of the pro-analysis in (22). The arguments in support of the pro-drop analysis for Igbo is outside the scope of this work. For details of the arguments, see the three works cited above.

(22)

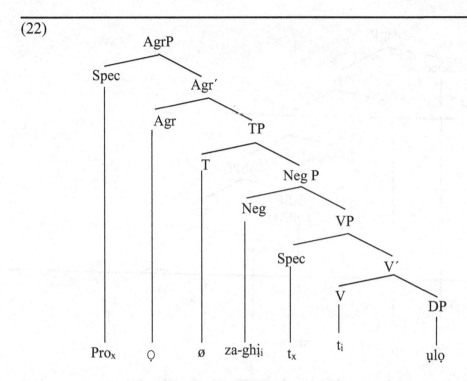

When the subject pronoun *m* and *ha* remain in-situ as we claimed in section 4.3.2.1, the *e-* verbal prefix occupies the Agr head position and serves as the syntactic 'subject' of the sentence. This is demonstrated with (23).

(23)   a.   À-za-ghì   hà ụlọ̀
                 AGR-sweep-NEG 3P house
                 'They did not sweep the house'

b.

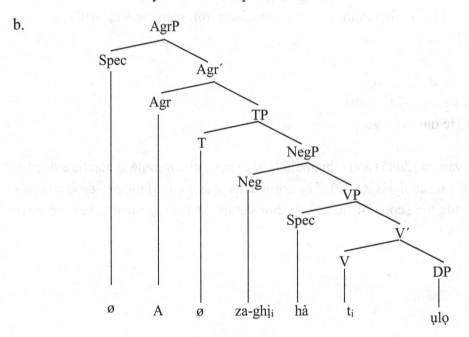

The presence of NegP automatically implies the presence TP. In fact, Zanuttini (1996: 181) rightly notes, "the functional category NegP is parasitic on the functional category TP". In other words, there can be no NegP without a TP. If Neg is dependent on T and T has scopal authority over V, then that explained why NegP (ie as a functional head) is a predicate operator in languages where it exists. Igbo has only NegP and for that reason no constituent of an Igbo sentence can be negated without involving the predicate. Constituent negation in Igbo involve cleftings, where the negated constituent is focused and introduced by a copula predicator such as *bụ* and *dị* as in (24b) or the verb *nwe* which translates as 'there is' as in (24a).

(24)   a.   Ò nwe-ghī onye zụrụ akwụkwọ ya
                  ES cop-NEG person buy-rV book   his
                  'Nobody bought his book'

      b.   Ò bụ-ghī Obi zùrù ụgbọàlà ahù
                  ES cop-NEG Obi buy-rV vehicle   that
                  'It is not Obi that bought that vehicle'

The constituents of the sentences, *Onye* and *Obi* are negated by the cleft constructions *O nweghi* and *O bughi*.

From the analysis we have done so far and supported by the theoretical assumption that tense is a universal category, we have seen that the functional category T is obligatory in every Igbo clause. Every verb strives to raise to T, but since movement is motivated by Greed, verbs without overt tense affixes do not overtly get to T. Those with strong tense features but no tense affix get an agreement support for the empty T position.

5.2 T-AGR-ASP-NEG Interactions

We have seen that there are interactions between Tense, Aspect and Negation in Igbo. We shall look at these interactions in negative perfective constructions and the negation-tense interaction marked by the tone patterns of the agreement prefix and that of the verb. We shall discuss these interactions under two subheadings: T-ASP-NEG interaction in Negative Perfective construction and T-AGR-NEG Interaction and tonal pattern.

5.2.1 T-ASP-NEG Interaction in Negative Perfective Construction

We have noted that ASP and NEG are two separate functional heads. We have shown in section 4.3.3.1 that perfective construction is negated by the general negative marker *ghi* plus *–be-*, giving the form *-beghi*. We have also argued that *-be-* is the negative suppletive form of *-la* in the affirmative. (25a-d) are examples of negative perfective constructions.

(25)   a.   Àda a-zā-bè-ghì   ụlọ̀
                Ada   AGR-sweep-PF-NEG house
                'Ada has not swept the house'

         b.   Ò   ri-bè-ghì   nri
                3S   eat-PF-NEG food
                'S/He has not eaten'

         c.   Ha e-gbū-bè-ghị̀   ọ̀kụkọ̀
                3P AGR-kill-PF-NEG fowl
                'They have not killed a fowl'

The sentences in (25) show that NEG, ASP and AGR are instantiated in negative perfective constructions. (25a), for example, has the following structure.

(26)

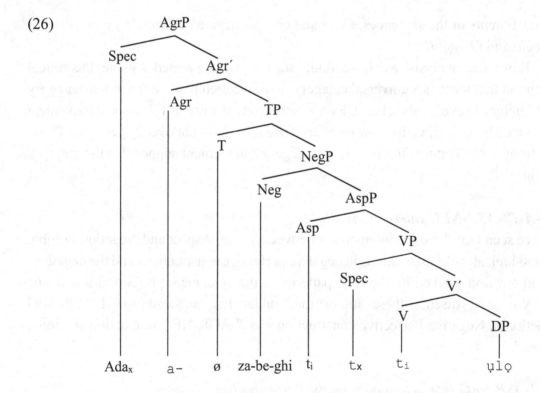

Why do we assume the hierachical order, T–Neg–Asp in (26)? The theoretical assumption is that the verb is built up in the lexicon with affixes, but it seems that the rule that combines the affixes with the verb within the lexicon is sensitive to the order of the functional categories in the syntax, such that the innermost suffix is that associated with the functional category closest to the verb in hierachical order. The perfective suffix is closer to the verb than the negative suffix. The perfective suffix *-be* attaches first before the negative suffix. If Asp should be higher than Neg, then it will yield the following unacceptable structure.

(27)   * a-za-ghi-be
          AGR-sweep-NEG-PF

The hierarchy in (26) implies that T c-commands and has scopal authority over NegP and all that it dominates. In the same vien, Neg c-commands AspP and VP. In (26), V raises first to Asp and then V + Asp raises to Neg. The complex V+Asp+Neg does not raise to T because there is no tense morpheme. As we have earlier observed, the agreement prefix gives support to the empty T position.

Emenanjo (1985:165) observes that in Nneewi and in many other dialects, 'in rapid speech the general negative marker *ho* can be elided when it follows *-be* without any change in meaning'. This is shown in (28) below.

(28)   Ọ̀ dụ-bè   mmā
              3S   be-PF.NEG goodness
              'It is not yet good'

Dechaine (1993) argues that *-be* is an Negative Polarity Item (NPI) since it can mark negation as in (28). A closer look at (28), shows that the speakers do not only elide the General Negative suffix but lengthen the vowel of *-be*. (28) is actually realised as (29).

(29)   Ọ̀ dụ-bè-è   mmā
              3S   be-PF-NEG goodness
              'It is not yet good'

In our own opinion, the vowel copy of *-be* is to indicate the missing negative suffix. The vowel copy bears the low tone of the elided negative suffix.

5.2.2 *T-AGR-NEG Interaction and Tonal Pattern*
We have shown in section 4.3.3.3, that tone plays a very important role in Igbo negation. The role of tone in Igbo negation can easily be seen in suffixless negative constructions. Consider the examples below from Nneewi dialect.

(30)   a.   Ike ya e-li   nni
                Ike ANT e-eat food
                'Ike will eat'

b.　　Ike a-yā　　　　　　e-li　nnī
　　　Ike AGR.NEG-ANT e-eat food
　　　'Ike will not eat'

(31)　a.　　Ọ　yà　è-bɔ ụrị̀à
　　　　　3S ANT e-cry cry
　　　　　'S/He will cry'

　　　b.　　Ọ̀ ya　　　　e-be　ụrị̀à
　　　　　3S ANT.NEG e-cry cry
　　　　　'S/He will not cry'

(32)　a.　　Àda nà a-zà　　unyò
　　　　　Ada DUR e-sweep house
　　　　　'Ada is sweeping the house'

　　　b.　　Àda a-hā　　　a-zà　unyò
　　　　　Ada AGR.NEG-DUR e-sweep house
　　　　　'Ada is not sweeping the house'

(33)　a.　　Ọ nà a-zà　unyò
　　　　　3S DUR e-sweep house
　　　　　'S/He is sweeping the house'

　　　b.　　Ọ̀ hā　　　a-zà　unyò
　　　　　3S NEG.DUR e-sweep house
　　　　　'S/He is not sweeping the house'

In the b examples in (30) – (33), negative meaning is expressed. In all of them, the negative suffix is missing. The agreement prefix occurs with non-clitic subjects as in (30b) and (32b). In (31b) and (33b), there is no agreement prefix and no negative suffix, yet negation is clearly implied. In (32) and (33), the auxiliary durative marker *na* changes to *ha* in the negative. In that case, *ha* is the negative suppletive form of *na*. However, the tone pattern of the durative negative remains the same with the anticipative in (30) and (31).

　　The data in (30)-(33) are particularly revealing. In all the instances where negative meaning is expressed, a high tone is found somewhere between the agreement prefix and the verbal element, in this case the auxiliary verbs. In (30b) and (32b), the agreement prefix bears a high tone which influences the inherent low tone of the auxiliary verb to raise to a downstep. In the absence of the agreement prefix, the auxiliary verb takes over the high tone as in (30b) and (33b). Ndimele (2009) argues that the low tone borne by the subject clitic pronoun in (31b) and (33b) is an indication that negation in Igbo is marked by a floating low tone. We have, in section 4.3.3.3, argued to the contrary. The tone of the subject pronoun has no role to play in Igbo negation. The same pronoun can bear a low tone in the interrogative construction. Moreover, there is no low tone in the environment where there is no subject clitic pronoun. This is unlike the interrogative low tone which could be found with non-clitic subjects as shown in (34) (also from Nneewi)

(34)   a.   Ọ̀   nà a-zà   unyò
                3S DUR e-sweep house
                'Is s/he sweeping the house?'

        b.   Àda à-nà   a-zà   unyò
                Ada AGR-DUR e-sweep house
                'Is Ada sweeping the house?'

Dechaine (1993) observes that the agreement prefix bears a high tone, but we have seen that the same agreement prefix can bear low tone if no negative meaning is implied. Even main verbs can sometimes be negated without the negative suffix as in (35) (adapted from Uwalaka 2003; 11, glossing is mine)

(35)   a.   A-mā   Jizọs bụ̀ ọrị̀à
                AGR.NEG-know Jesus be sickness
                'The lack of knowledge of Jesus is sickness'

        b.   Madụ̀ a-mā   Jizọs bụ̀ ọrị̀à
                person AGR.NEG-know Jesus be sickness
                'For a person not to know Jesus is sickness'

In (35a & b), the agreement element bears a high tone. This high tone marks negation and influences the low tone (which most verbs bear in simple declarative sentences, irrespective of their inherent tone pattern) of the main verb *ma* 'know' to become a downstep. This is why we gloss the agreement prefix as AGR.NEG.

Another evidence in support of the role of high tone in Igbo negation, could be found in Igbo personal names. Igbo personal names provide good examples of economy in language. Most names are clausal in structure but made as short as possible, ensuring that the intended meanings are not lost. There are Igbo names that carry negative meaning,[6] but do not occur with negative suffix. For example, *Ife anyịghị Chukwu* meaning, 'Nothing is too difficult for God' is rendered *Ifeanyichukwu. Amaghi nna* with the literal meaning 'One does not know father' is rendered *Amanna*. The morphemic make-up of the two names are shown in (36).

(36)   a.   Ife-a-nyị̀-chukwu
                thing-AGR.NEG-surpass-God
                'Nothing surpasses God'

        b.   A-ma-nnà
                AGR.NEG-know-father
                'One who does not know the father'

There is no negative suffix in (36a & b). But the high tone borne by the agreement prefix gives the names their negative reading. The indicative low tone of *ma* changes to a step tone which is an indication of an underlying high tone. A change in the tone pattern of (36b) for example will give different readings to the name.

(37)   a.   A-mà-nnà
                AGR-know-father
                'The father is known'   (affirmative)

        b.   À-mà-nnà
                AGR-know-father
                'Is the father known?'   (interogative)

(37) shows that an interrogative could be differentiated from non-interrogatve by a low tone on the subject pronoun (in (37) an agreement prefix, traditionally referred to as impersonal pronoun). Since the affirmative (non-interogative) bears a high tone subject pronoun (in this case, prefix), the high tone of negation has to flop to the following verb, forcing an inherently low tone verb to bear a downstep tone (37b).

    Our analysis shows that negation is jointly marked by the suffix *ghi* and high tone borne by some other element in a higher c-commanding position in Igbo. The fact that negation can be expressed only with tone is an indication that high tone plays a more important role in Igbo negation than the negative suffix. The *e-* agreement prefix which normally bears high tone in negative construction is therefore a joint spell-out of stranded T and Neg. The segmental morpheme belongs to T/Agr, while the prosodic

---

[6] Here we are referring to syntactic negation. There is the pragmatic assumption that certain names have negative connotations.

morpheme belongs to Neg. This is possible because T c-commands NegP in Igbo and so the features of Neg can percolate to T. Zanuttini's (1996) proposal on the dependence of NegP on TP, lends support to the T and Neg interaction on the *e-* prefix. This is why we gloss the *e-* high tone prefix in negative constructions as 'AGR.NEG'. The tree diagram in (38) shows how the high tone of Neg percolates to Agr.

(38)

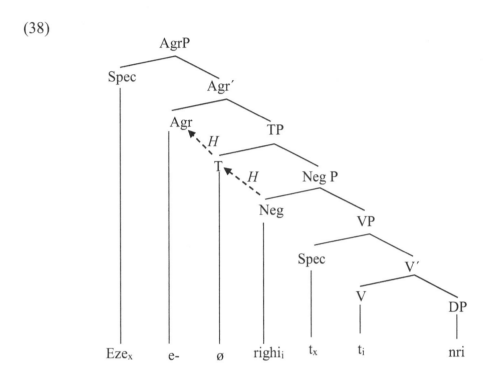

The broken arrows in (38) are to show that the high tone is generated under Neg. The high tone percolated to T, but since T is empty, it percolates further to the overt segmental agreement morpheme.

5.3   An Articulated Structure for the Igbo Verbal Functional Categories

From the discussion and analysis in this chapter, it appears that Agreement, Tense, Aspect and Negation are morphologically marked in Igbo. Agreement appears in form of a default element where T is empty. Tense has an overt realisation only in the past. Aspect and Negation are clearly marked in the language. Following the UG assumption, we take it that AgrP and TP are obligatorily projected in Igbo whether they have morphological content or not.

We therefore assume the hierarchical order of AGR-T-NEG-ASP-V. The articulated clause structure for Igbo is shown in 108. In 108, all the positions: Specifier, Head and Complement are shown.

(39)

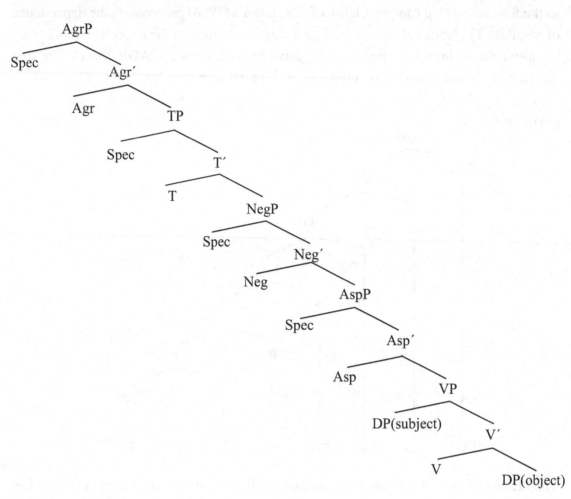

5.4 Summary

In this chapter, we gave theoretical analysis of the Igbo verbal functional categories. We showed that the functional heads Agr, T, Asp and Neg are present in Igbo. We differ from Uwalaka (2003), in positing separate TP and ASPP. V-movement to tense occurs if there is a past tense morpheme, otherwise V moves only to Asp and Neg leaving T empty. The empty T position is normally supported by a default agreement prefix which is found in negative and perfective constructions. The extension of the default agreement analysis to the prefix in perfective construction is a modification of Dechaine's Neg-barrier analysis. We propose that an empty T with strong tense features is what triggers off default agreement. We also observed that in negative constructions, the agreement prefix bears a high tone which we have analysed as the more important negative marker.

In the next chapter, we shall look at yet another important functional category, this time not associated with the verb but with the noun, the determiner.

Chapter 6
Functional Categories in the Igbo Nominal Domain

6.0 Preliminaries

Determiner (abbreviated to Det in earlier works and to D in more recent works) is a functional element or functor which is defined by Radford (1997:447) as 'a word which is typically used to modify a noun, but which has no descriptive content of its own'. Determiner is a traditional notion used to refer to nominal modifiers such as articles, demonstratives, quantifiers, etc., that determine the referential or quantificational properties of the nouns associated with them. If we assume determiners to be functional categories, then they should have the characteristics that define functional categories which include among others

- lack of descriptive content
- limited in number (closed class)
- morphological dependency (affixes, clitics)
- sometimes null (empty category)

(cf. Abney 1987)

It is important to note that sometimes certain functional categories appear as independent lexical items. Determiner seems to belong to this group. In some languages, it exists in the form of an independent lexical item, in some, it appears in the form of an affix attached to the noun and yet in many other languages, it appears as a null constituent of the nominal phrase. To this last group belongs Igbo. We shall demonstrate in this study that Igbo lacks determiner as it exists in languages like English, but yet projects a determiner phrase (henceforth DP) which is headed by a null category or by a special link item *nke* which optionally occurs in all types of Igbo nominal expressions.

6.1 Defining the Igbo Determiner

Progovac (1995) is of the view that, articles such as the English 'the' and 'a' are the only elements that could be said to be true determiners. In line with Progovac's view, Adger (2003) identifies determiners in English as elements that are in complementary distribution with the definite article 'the'. These elements include the indefinite article 'a', demonstratives: this, that, and quantifiers: all, every, etc. These elements do not co-occur with 'the' as demonstrated by the ungrammaticality of (1a-c).

(1)   a.   *the a teacher
           b.   *this the book
           c.   *the every book

The fact, that these other modifiers do not co-occur with the articles led to the classification of all such nominal pre-modifiers as determiners in English.

Igbo has no definite or indefinite articles. However, these other nominal modifiers: demonstrative, quantifier, adjective exist in Igbo. The question is, do they qualify to be called determiners in Igbo? Mbah (2006: 112) contends that the "Igbo language does not have determiners as it is used in the Indo-European languages in association with common nouns". He rather prefers to use the term 'determiner' to refer to any category in Igbo "which qualifies, modifies or quantifies a head so as to discriminate it from other hitherto identical lexical items". Going by Mbah's definition of Igbo determiners, all nominal modifiers, including adjectives, relative clauses, possessive NPs are all determiners. We disagree with Mbah on this non-technical use of determiner for two reasons. One, determiners are functional categories and functional categories generally lack descriptive content. Adjectives, possessive NPs and relative clauses do not lack descriptive or thematic content and therefore do not qualify as functional categories in Igbo. Two, if we take all Igbo nominal modifiers to be determiners, then, there is no node in the phrase that could be seen as dominating and c-commanding all the other nodes within the nominal phrase since many of them, unlike the English determiners can co-occur. Consider (2) below

(2)   ụlọ̀   ahụ̀ niilē buru ibū
                 house Dem Q   RC
                 'all those houses that are big

If we take (Dem)onstrative, (Q)uantifier and R(elative) C(lause) to be determiners, then (2) will be a case of a nominal phrase with non-projecting modifiers, which is undesirable from a theoretical perspective (See Modifier Maximality Constraint, Stowell, 1981) .

Our position here is that Igbo generally lacks an overt determiner. But, the D head position could be occupied by *ǹkè* which is a functional element that could optionally occur in any type of Igbo nominal construction. The modifiers project separate functional or lexical categories such as DemP, GenP, QP, AP etc). Our position hinges on the DP-Hypothesis. Before we explore the DP hypothesis can apply to Igbo, let us look at the constituents of the Igbo nominal phrase.

6.2 Constituents of the Igbo Nominal Phrase

Elements of different categories could be found within an Igbo nominal phrase. These elements co-occur with some degree of flexibility in the word order that co-relates with slight meaning differences or no difference at all. The examples in (3a & b) are acceptable structures in Igbo.

(3) a. ụlọ̀ ahụ̀ dum̀
      house Dem Q
      'all those houses'

    b. ụlọ̀ dum̀ ahụ̀
      house Q   Dem
      'all those houses'

(3a & b) show that a demonstrative and a quantifier can exchange position without bringing about change in meaning. Basically, Noun is the first element within the Igbo nominal phrase as seen in (3) above. However, there are marked cases where the modifier comes before the noun as shown in (4).

(4) a. otù nwokē
      one man
      'one man'

    b. ajọ̄ mmadụ̀
      bad person
      'bad person'

    c. ogologo osisi
      tallness tree
      'tall tree'

    d. nnukwu ụlọ̀
      bigness house
      'big house'

It is important to note that these premodifiers have postmodifying equivalents. Except for the numeral *otù* 'one', and some other units of Igbo traditional counting system such as, *ohū/ọgū* 'twenty', *nnù* 'forty', all other numerals are postmodifiers.

(5) a. otù onyē   b. * onye otù
      one person   person one
      'one person'

(6)   a.   ohu   mmadụ̀   b.   ? m̀madụ̀ ohù
              twenty person   person twenty
              'twenty people'

(7)   a.   * àbụ̀ọ mmadụ   b.   m̀madụ̀ àbụ̀ọ
              two person   person two
                                           'two people'

(8)   a.   * ìse mmadụ̀   b.   m̀madụ̀ ìse
              five person   person five
                                           'five people'

94b-d) have postmodifying equivalents as shown in (9).

(9)   a.   mmadụ̀ ọjọ̄ọ̄
                  person bad
                  'bad person'

             b.   osisi ogologo
                  tree   tallness
                  'tall tree'

             c.   ụlọ̀ nnukwū/ukwu
                  house bigness/big
                  'big house'

Mbah (2006) argues that Igbo is strictly head-initial and that within nominal phrases, nouns are the heads. He therefore argues that lexemes such as *ajọ* and *nnukwu* in 4b and 4d respectively are heads. According to him, 'the initial lexemes are heads rather than prenominal modifiers. ... but as attributes ..., they obligatorily require entities to be attributed to'. Head being initial is supported in the literature (cf. Kayne 1994, Longobardi 1994), But, for Mbah to argue that *ajọ/ogologo/nnukwu* are heads in (4) while the same lexemes: *ọjọọ/ogologo/ukwu* are modifiers in (9) is not plausible. We do not see any difference in meaning between the two groups of expressions. Though, it is possible to use a noun such as *ogologo* as a head noun as shown in (10), It does not have the same status as in (4c). In (4c) and (9b), *ogologo* is the modifier, the word order notwithstanding.

(10)   ogologo Obì dì egwù
             tallness Obi be fear
             'Obi's tallness is wonderful'

The difference in word order, as examplified by (4) and (9), shows that movement is possible within the Igbo nominal phrase. We shall, in section 6.4 show what moves and to where.

We also observe that the other modifiers occur to the right of N. Consider (11).

(11)   a. akwụkwọ ukwu ahụ̀
              book   big   Dem
              'that big book'

       b. nwanyì ọma   à
              woman beautiful Dem
              'this beautiful woman'

       c. ụlọ̀   ha   niile
              house their Q
              'all their houses'

The Demonstrative or the Quantifier seems to be the last element within the nominal phrase. Change in word order leads to ungrammaticality as demonstrated by 12.

(12)   a. * akwụkwọ ahụ̀ ukwu
              book   Dem big

       b. *nwanyì à   ọma
             woman Dem beautiful

       c. *ụlọ̀   niile ha
             house Q   their

Brugè (1997) argues that the demonstrative must be generated in a low position in Spanish, given the fact that the demonstrative *este* 'that' can follow the noun and its modifiers. We adopt this analysis for Igbo as well, and argue that there is a separate category Dem and a separate category Q which contrary to the surface word order c-commands the NP. It is higher up in the structure than the NP. It then means that the NP together with its adjectival modifier moves to a higher position and appear before the demonstrative and the quantifier.

Emenanjo (1978:80) gives a rough schematic representation of the structure of a simple[1] nominal phrase showing all the possible constituents.

(13) $\pm$A $\Big\}$ $\underbrace{+N \pm A \pm P \pm Nm \pm Q \pm D \pm Q}$ $\pm$ $\Big\{$ RC

          Head   Central

Note:

$\pm$	= Optional	Nm	= Numeral
+	= Obligatory	Q	= Quantifier
A	= Adjective	D	= Demonstrative
N	= Noun	RC	= Relative Clause
P	= Pronominal Modifier		

What Emenanjo is trying to show in (13) is that the Igbo nominal phrase could contain different types of categories which are optional and do co-occur. As expected, the only obligatory constituent is the Noun which is assumed to be the head of the phrase. (14) below is an illustrative phrase where all the constituents in (13) are present.

(14)   ajọ akwà ọcha ānyị atọ niilē ahù furu èfù[2]
          A   N   A   P   Nm Q   D   RC
          'all those three bad white clothes of ours that are missing'

(14) shows that different types of modifiers can co-occur in the same NP.

6.3 Igbo Nominal Phrase and the DP Hypothesis

We have discussed, in chapter two, section 2.4.2, the theoretical assumptions of the DP hypothesis. The DP hypothesis does not suggest that the maximal projection NP does not exist, Rather, it claims that the determiner is the head of a higher functional projection DP headed by a functional element D which takes NP as its complement. It then means that NP itself is headed by N. The DP hypothesis claims that it is the DP that occupies the argument positions (subject, object, etc) in a clause. This is irrespective of whether there is overt D element in the phrase or not.

This brings us to the contention by Mbah (1999, 2006) that the noun is the head of NP in Igbo because it is the only obligatory element within the Igbo Noun Phrase.

---

[1] It is not clear why Emenanjo prefers to refer to the structure as simple since the schema contains also a relative clause.

[2] This structure might sound a bit odd for some Igbo speakers because of the premodifying adjective ajọ which has a postmodifying alternative ọjọọ. We only use the structure to show how Emenanjo's schema can be instantiated

Yes, the noun is obligatory within the Igbo Noun phrase but that does not imply that a head cannot be covert. D is a head, but it can have a zero realisation.

English and some other languages have overt elements, such as articles, demonstratives, genitive 's, that could occupy the D head position. This brings up the question, whether languages like Igbo, where no article exists and Nouns occur before the functional elements, project DPs as proposed in the theory. We will demonstrate in this chapter that in addition to the functional category Dem, Gen and Q in Igbo, there is a functional category D which is higher up in the structure, c-commands and has scopal authority over the NP and the other functional categories within the phrase. This functional category D may appear null or occupied by a lexical element *ǹkè* which optionally occurs with any of the other functional elements.

Based on the DP hypothesis, we propose the structure in (15) for Igbo.

(15)

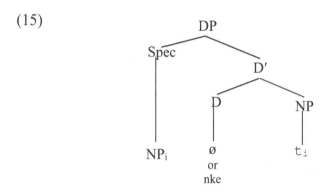

We assume the structure in (15) following the Linear Correspondence Axiom (LCA) proposed by Kayne (1994). We shall define LCA and explore its applicability to the Igbo nominal phrase in the next section.

6.4 Functional Heads, Word Order and the Directionality Parameter within the Igbo Nominal Phrase

If we adopt the DP-hypothesis for Igbo, which assumes that the argument nominal phrase is headed by a functional element, the structures where the noun comes before the functional element present a problem for a theory that assumes the functional head to be higher in the structure and have scope over the NP which it c-commands. Consider the phrases below.

(16) a. ụlọ̀ niilē   c. nwokē ọcha ahụ̀
          house Q   man fair Dem
          'all houses'   'that fair man'

      b. mmadụ̀ duṁ   d. òke à
          person Q   rat Dem
          'everybody'   'this rat'

In (16), the functional elements: Dem and Q appear after the nouns and therefore lower in the structure. On the contrary, the DP-hypothesis assumes the functional elements to be higher in the structure to be able to c-command the NP. How then do we account for the 'deviant' Igbo structures in (16)? Kayne (1994) claims that "Heads must always precede their associated complement position, even though in some languages the surface order may be Head-Complement (H-C) and in some others Complement-Head (C-H). In languages with the C-H order, Kayne proposes that the complement undergoes left adjunction to the specifier position. This proposal makes the claim that the universal ordering between a head and its dependents is Specifier-Head-Complement (S-H-C). Kayne (1994) refers to this proposal as the Linear Correspondence Axiom (LCA) represented in (17).

(17)

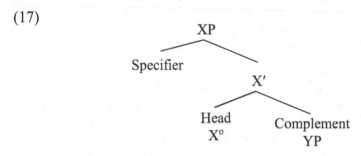

If Kayne's proposal is correct, then structures such as 16 could be analysed as being headed by functional heads that take NPs as their complements. The NP complement moves to the Spec position in surface syntax giving rise to the C-H order. This is illustrated in (18) below.

(18)

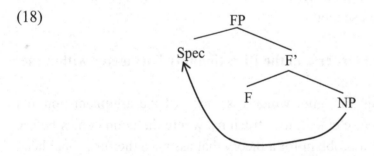

(16a), for example, will have the structure in (19).

(19)

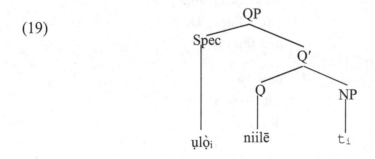

(19) shows that N moves into its surface position where it appears before the quantifier. There are two possibilities. The N head could move to the head of the functional category (head to head movement) or the NP could move to the Spec position of the functional projection. Since Igbo does not show any form of agreement morphology between the noun and the associated functional category, we assume the latter for Igbo as shown in (18) and (19). We assume that in addition to the projection of a functional category D, which in most cases has zero realisation in Igbo (since Igbo lacks an overt determiner), there are other functional heads such as Dem, Q, Gen which the D head c-commands. (16c) could be analyzed as having the structure in (20).

(20)

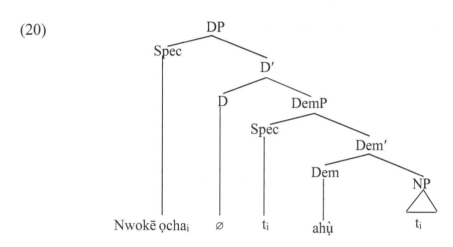

Our analysis here is similar to that done for Javanese and Madurese by Davies and Dresser (2005). These languages also exhibit demonstrative final position. The same analysis was used by Bernstein (1997) for German. Our analysis differs from that of Davies and Dresser (2005) in assuming that it is the NP that moves to the Spec of DP, unlike in Javanese and Madurese where the N head moves to the D head. The difference is because Javanese and Madurese have overt D morphemes that agree with the noun. Igbo has none. The Javanese and Madurese data below are from Davies & Dresser (2005:61)

(21)   a.   kucing-è nyolong iwak   (Javanese)
                 cat-DEF AV.steal fish
                 'The cat stole (some) fish'

        b.   koceng-nga ngeco' juko'   (Madurese)
                 cat-DEF AV.steal fish
                 'The cat stole (some) fish'

The fact that in Igbo, N moves with its adjectival modifier as shown in (20) indicates that it is the whole NP that moves and not only the head N. This could explain why (22) is not grammatical.

(22)   *Nwokē ahụ̀ ọcha
             Man   that fair

(20) assumes that the NP *nwokē ọcha* moves from the complement position, first to Spec DemP and further to Spec DP. In the course of the movement, the NP acquires the features of the functional heads and so could be interpreted as [+ definite + specific].

More than one functional projection could be found within the Igbo nominal phrase, since the functional elements can co-occur. Examine (23) below.

(23)

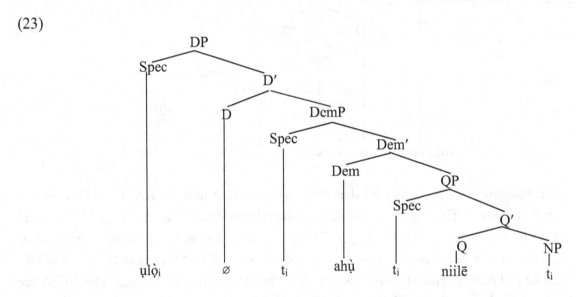

There is no hierarchical order between the DemP and QP. Any of them can dominate the other as shown by the acceptability of both (3a & b) above in section 6.2. By the movement of the NP to the Spec of the available functional projections, the noun has equal access to the features of the functional heads in a spec-head relationship. For example, the Q *niilē* assigns the feature [+ plural] to the N, while the Dem *ahụ̀* assigns the features [+ definite + specific]. This could explain why the NP *ụlọ̀* could be interpreted as definite and as plural without any overt plural marker.

The question that might arise is, to explain why we assume a separate D head different from Dem and Q in (23). The answer to this question could be given by looking at three issues: the structure of the Igbo genitive phrase, the position of *ǹkè* in the Igbo nominal phrase and the semantic interpretation of bare nominals.

6.5 Igbo Genitive Constructions

Genitive seems to be a cover term for possessive and associative[3] constructions. Anyanwu (1996:77) defines an associative construction as 'a construction which links two or more nouns (e.g noun1-noun2- (noun3)) to form, for instance, a genitive phrase'. She uses the term associative construction to refer to both association and possession. She uses 'specific' and 'non-specific' to distinguish the two. According to her:

> The Associative Construction [specific] can easily be contrasted with the Associative Construction [non-specific] in that the second noun N2 in the Associative Construction [specific] is a proper or personified name. Furthermore, the Associative Construction [specific] has a specific reference as opposed to the generic reference of Associative Construction [non-specific] (p. 77)

Anyanwu's distinction between Associative Construction [specific] and Associative Construction [non-specific] corresponds to the traditional distinction between possession and association. This is shown in (24). In Igbo, both the possessive and the associative constructions appear as noun-noun constructions where the second noun modifies the first one.

(24)   a.   ego ụzọ̀
                money road
                'road fare'

           b.   ego Ùzọ̀
                money Name
                'Mr Ụzọ's money'

The distinction between the two types of constructions is sometimes viewed as a distinction between alienable and inalienable possession. Ownership is seen as alienable possession while association is seen as inalienable possession. We shall, following Anyanwu (1996) refer to the two types of constructions in (24) as Genitve Constructions. However, it is important to note that the two types of constructions have different tone patterns as shown by the (a) and (b) pairs in (25)-(27).

(25)   a.   ụlọ̄ Ēgō   b.   ụlọ̀ egō
                house P. name   house money
                'Ego's house'   'bank'

---

[3] Associative constructions are sometimes treated as nominal compounds

(26)   a.   isi   Ānyā   b.   isi   anyā
              head P. name   head eye
              'Anya's head'   'the corner of the eye'

(27)   a.   àla   Īkē   b.   àlà   ikē
              land P. name   land strength
              'Ike's land'   'hard surface'

The tone patterns observed in (25)-(27) are shown in table VIII below.

Table VIII: Tone patterns in some Igbo genitive constructions

Data No	Inherent tone		Ownership or Alienable Possession (a)	Association or Inalienable possession (b)
	NP1	NP2		
25	H L	H S	H S S S	H L H S
26	H H	II H	H H S S	H H H S
27	L L	H H	L H S S	L L H S

What is common between the two types of constructions is that there are predictable tonal changes to reflect the relationship between N1 and N2[4]. In (27), for example, where the NP1 *ala* has a LL tone pattern, the last low has to raise to high to be able to provide the appropriate tonal environment for a downstep. Tone is therefore a genitive marker in Igbo. We can then posit a Genitive Phrase (GenP) in Igbo and tone as its exponent. The tone pattern is influenced by the inherent tones of the nouns as well as the alienable and inalienable distinction shown in (25)-(27) above.

The genitive construction establishes a relation between two nouns: the possessor and the possessum. Kayne (1994), Cinque (2003), among others assumes that an abstract head mediates the relationship between the two arguments. Ajiboye (2007) proposes a 'small clause' headed by small v as the base structure of Yoruba genitive phrases. He defines a small clause as 'a defective nominal or verbal clause containing two arguments and a relational head that may but need not be pronounced' (p. 27). With the small clause analysis he is able to uniformly account for nominal and verbal genitives. Ajiboye (2007) further states that when the vP is a defective nominal clause, v is null, but when it is a verbal clause, v is realised as a possessive verb. The structure proposed by Ajiboye (2007) for Yoruba is shown in (28).

---

[4] For details of these tone patterns, see Nwachukwu (1995)

(28)

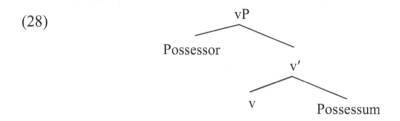

Within the Yoruba nominal phrase, the possessum precedes the possessor.

(29)   a.   ìwé   e   Túndé
                book MTS Tunde
                'Tunde's book'

          b.   bàbá   a   Túndé
                father MTS Tunde
                'Tunde's father'

          c.   apá   a   Túndé
                arm MTS Tunde
                'Tunde's arm'

(from Ajiboye, 2007:30)

Ajiboye identifies a Mid Tone Syllable (MTS) which is a vowel copy of the possessum NP as the element that shows the relation between the two NPs. He goes further to anlayze the nominal genitive construction as being dominated by a higher functional projection DP, where the MTS occurs in the head D position and the possessum NP moves from the complement position of v to the spec of DP. We have earlier noted that Ajiboye assumes that the head v is null in nominal genitives. This is shown in (30).

(30)

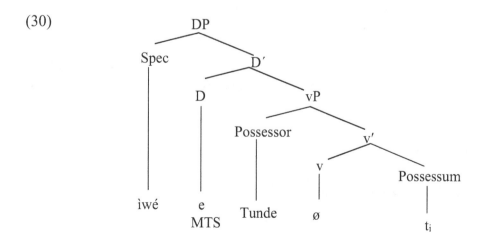

In Igbo, we argue instead for a GenP which relates the possessor to the possessum. The genitive marker, in form of tone is the mediator between the two arguments and establishes an R-relation between them. Tone could be said to occupy the Gen head position while the D head is null. (25a) could be analyzed as in (31).

(31)

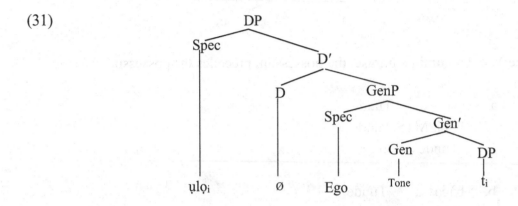

In (31), Tone in the Gen head position links the possessor DP to its possessum DP complement. The movement of the DP possessum to the spec of the higher DP spreads the tonal effect to the other syllables producing the surface tone patterns observed in (25)-(27). The GenP in (31) has a parallel structure in the verbal genitive shown in (32).

(32)   a.   Egō   nwè   ụlọ̀
             Ego   own   house
             'Ego owns the house'

b.

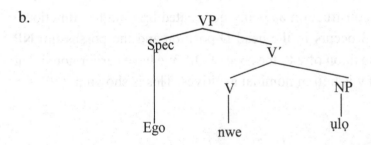

Evidence for the analysis of the possessum DP as having moved from the complement position to the Spec position comes from relative clauses involving possession as in (33) below.

(33)   a.   ụlọ̀   Egō   nwè
                house   Ego   own
                'the house that Ego owns'

b.

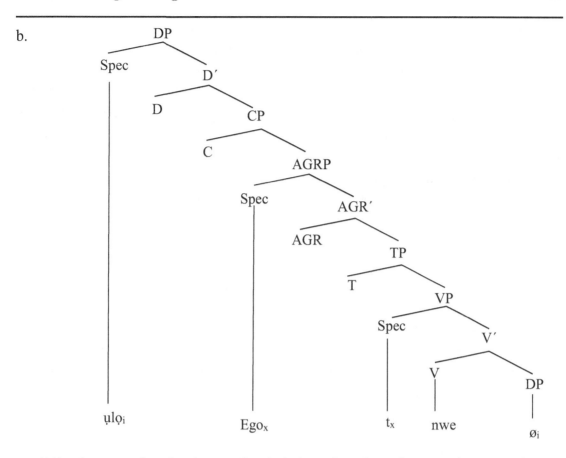

In (33), the DP *ulo+Ø* takes a CP (relative clause) as its complement. The DP complement of the verb nwe is deleted because it is co-referential with the subject of the main clause *ulo*. In other words, the relativized DP is the object of the verb. The non-realisation of the object is traditionally treated as Equi-NP deletion. *Ulo* in the Spec DP is the subject of the main clause which is modified by the embedded relative clause. *Ego* in (33) is in the subject position of the modifying relative clause (Spec AGRP), unlike in (31) where it occupies the subject (Spec GenP) position of a Genitive Phrase. Possession in (33) is marked by the verb of ownership *nwe*. In this case, tone is not the marker of possession and that could explain why *ulò* and *Egō* retained their inherent tone in (33a).

6.6 *Ǹkè*: An Optional D Head

Another evidence in support of a different D head from other functional heads in Igbo is the occurrence of *ǹkè* with virtually all types of nominal modifiers. Consider (34).

(34) a. ulō ǹke Ego   c. ulò ǹkè ano
    house ? Ego   book ? Nm
    'Ego's house'   'the fourth house'

b.	akwà ǹke à		d. ụlọ̄ ǹkè ọcha
	cloth ? Dem		house ? white
	'this cloth'		'the white house'

What is the function of *ǹkè* in the examples above? *Ǹkè* seems to function like the definite determiner 'the' in English. For example, while *ụlọ̀ ọcha* could be interpreted as 'white house' or 'a white house', *ụlọ̄ ǹkè ọcha* must be interpreted as 'the white house'. The same thing is applicable to 34c where *ǹkè* is used with the ordinal numeral. The cardinal and ordinal number is distinguished by tone pattern.

(35)   a.   ụlọ̀   ànọ   b. ụlọ̄   anọ
                house four   house four
                'four houses'   'fourth house'

Ǹkè can occur with the ordinal number as in (34c). When it occurs, it carries with it some note of definiteness and specificity which is implicit with ordinal numbers. The definiteness and specificity features associated with *ǹkè* shows that it is a determiner. It can co-occur with other functional heads as shown by (34b) and (34c). (34b) can be analyzed as (36).

(36)

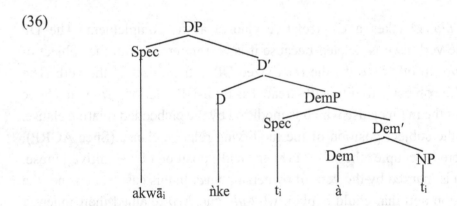

(36) shows that a DP headed by nke can take a DemP as complement. The NP which serves as the complement of the Dem first moves to Spec DemP and then to Spec DP given rise to the word order NP D Dem.

The same *nke* in (36) can be seen in genitive construction as shown in (37).

(37)

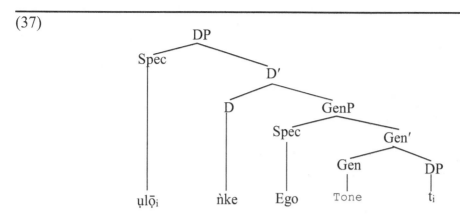

The presence of *nke* in (37) adds some note of specificity to the genitive construction. Structures such as (37), led Mbah (2006) to describe *ǹkè* as a possessive marker. It is not actually a possessive marker, since the same genitive tone pattern is observed with or without *ǹkè*. *Ǹkè* marks definiteness and specificity which are features of a determiner.

Another interesting reason why we assume *ǹkè* to be a true determiner is that it can be used as a pronoun. Abney (1987), Longobardi (2004) and Radford (2004), among others suggest that pronouns are determiners. The fact that pronouns could be used (as in English) to pronominally modify a following noun just like the other determiners: the, a, some, etc (as shown in (38)), led Radford (2004:47) to conclude that they are pronominal determiners

(38)   a.   [The republicans] don't trust [the democrats]
        b.   [We republicans] don't trust [you democrats]
        c.   [We] don't trust [you]

Following Radford (2004), we can argue that *ǹkè* can be used postnominally as well as pronominally.

(39)   a.   [ụlọ̀ ǹke à] bùrù ibù   (postnominal)
              house D Dem be bigness
              'this house is big'

        b.   [Ǹke à]   bùrù ibù   (pronominal)
              D Dem be   bigness
              'This is big'

In (39b), the NP complement of D *nke* is missing. In this case, *nke* is pronominal where it is modified by another functional head, Dem. Only nominal elements can be modified by demonstratives. *Nke* as a pronominal determiner stands in place of the NP and so could be modified by a demonstrative.

Uwalaka (1991:11) argues that *ǹkè,* found in the Igbo relative clause, is a relative complementizer which is equivalent to 'that' in English relative clause. Consider the following examples.

(40)   a.   [DP Àla ǹkè Ibē zụ̀rụ̀] adị̄ghị̄ mmā
            'The land that Ibe bought is not good'

       b.   [DP Ụlọ̄ ǹkè Òbi nwè] bùrù ibù
            'The house obi owns is big'

       c.   [DP Ụlọ̄ ǹke dara àdà] bụ̀ ǹkè m
            'The house that fell is mine'

We are contending that *ǹkè* in (40) is a D and not a C as claimed by Uwalaka (1991). However, *ǹkè* seems to be multi-functional. It can be used as a complementizer in negative sentences as demonstrated in (41).

(41)   a.   Ò nwe-ghī nne   ǹkè ọ nà è-nwe nnà
            3S own-NEG mother   C   3S AUX *e*-own father
            'He neither have a mother nor a father'

       b.   Òbi a-dī-ghī   ọcha ǹkè ọ nà à-di oji
            Obi AGR-be-NEG white C   3S AUX *e*-be black
            'Obi is neither fair nor dark'

       c.   Ụsụ a-bụ̄-ghī   anụ elū ǹkè ọ nà à-bụ anụ   àlà
            bat AGR-be-NEG animal up C   3S AUX *e*-be animal ground
            'A bat is neither a bird nor a ground animal'

In (41), *ǹkè* serves a coordinating conjunction between two negative clauses. Here, *ǹkè* is a complementizer which introduces only negative sentences. Interestingly, the negative clause introduced by *ǹkè* has no segmental negative marker. The negative marker in the first clause has scope over the second clause. Its negative meaning is derived from the main clause and the negative tone pattern of the subject and verbal element of the subordinate clause (See chapter five 5.1.3 for a discussion of negative tone pattern). *Nke* does not introduce affirmative clauses as shown by the unacceptablity of (42).

(42)   *Ụsu bụ̀ anụ elū ǹkè ọ bụ̀ anụ   àlà
            bat be animal up C   3S be animal ground

Nke, therefore can function as a determiner as well as a negative complementizer. It seems to me that the two are different. They are mere coincidents and therefore one of the many homonyms in the Igbo language. (40b) is therefore analyzed as a DP where *ǹkè* occupies the D head position.

(43)

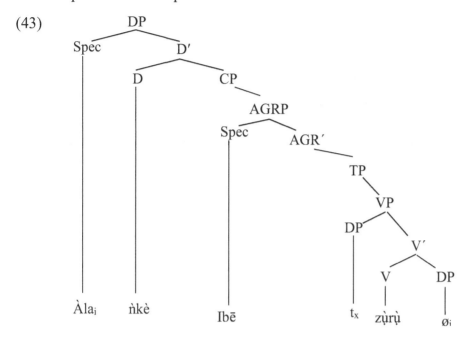

(43) is an object relative clause, i.e. a relative clause where the object is missing in its base generated position. A subject relative clause such as 40c will have the structure below.

(44)

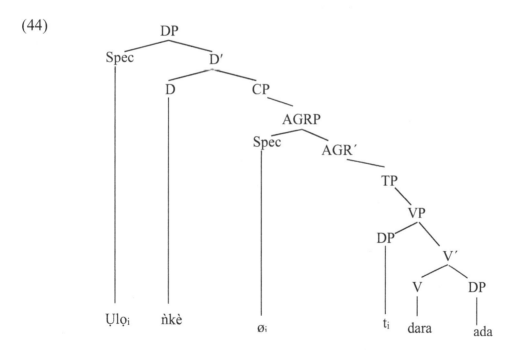

(43) and (44) show that the relativised DP is missing within the relative clause. The DP in the Spec of the higher DP is the focused subject which is modified by the embedded

relative clause (CP). *Nke* links the DP subject with the CP relative clause modifier. *Nke* is, therefore, the head of the higher DP. Our conclusion is that *ǹkè* is a D in the Igbo relative clauses.

6.7 Semantic Interpretation of Bare Nominals

Another reason for positing a null determiner head for Igbo has to do with the construal of bare nominals as definite, indefinite or generic. Bare nominals are common in Igbo sentences, but despite the bareness, they could be interpreted as definite, indefinite or generic, features associated with determiners in languages where they occur. The interpretation is context-dependent. Consider (45).

(45)   a.   Obi   nwèrè   aturū   (indefinite)
              Obi   own   sheep
              'Obi owns a sheep'

        b.   Nnà   m   nà   à-kpa aturū   (generic)
              father 1SgGEN AUX e-rear sheep
              'My father rears sheep'

        c.   Aturū   fù-rù   è-fù   (definite)
              sheep   be-lost e-lose
              'The sheep is lost'

The underlined nominal *aturū* could be construed as indefinite in (45a) because the context of utterance does not suggest that its referent is already familiar. Matthewson (1998) defines a noun as definite if it is familiar at the current stage of the conversation. The context that led to the utterance of (45a) does not suggest that *aturū* is already familiar to the addressee. Compare (45a) with (45c) where the utterance suggests that the listener is already familiar with a particular sheep which is reported missing. (45b) is generic. *Aturū* in (45b) refers to a kind in a group of animals. English does not allow bare nominals in the context of the Igbo examples above. The parallel examples in (46) from English are ungrammatical.

(46)   a.   * Obi has sheep
        b.   * Sheep is missing

English nouns require overt determiners to be grammatical. Such overt determiners mark them as either definite or indefinite. Igbo is not alone in expressing bare nominals. Yoruba, a close sister of Igbo and Japanese, among others, attest to bare nominals as shown in (47) and (48).

(47)   Yoruba (Ajíbóyè 2007:116)

      a.   Mo ri ajá   (indefinite)

           1Sg see dog

           'I saw a dog'

      b.   Aja gbó mi   (definite in discourse context)

           dog bark 1Sg

           'The dog barked at me'

(48)   Japanese (adapted from Fukui 1995: 105)

      a.   John-ga   hon-o   yonda

           John-NOM book-ACC read

           'John read a book'

      b.   <u>Inu-ga</u>   heya-ni   haitte-kita

           dog-NOM room-to in come-PAST

           'The dog entered the room

Bare nominals can be interpreted as definite, indefinite or generic which are features associated with the functional category D. This leads to the conclusion that in such languages including Igbo where there are bare nominals, there is an associated null D head which carries the D-features. For example, *aturu* in (45a) will have the structure (49).

(49)

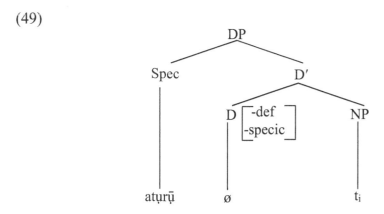

6.8   Summary

This chapter has tries to examine most of the elements that could be found within the Igbo nominal phrase. In line with the DP-hypothesis which assumes that a nominal phrase is headed by a functional element D, and the assumption that only elements that behave like articles are qualified to occupy the D head position, we conclude that Igbo does not have overt determiners like we have in English. Rather, Igbo has null D head. Evidence for the null head comes from the structure of genitival constructions involving noun-noun constructions that lack overt relational item. The tonal melody triggered by 'Tone', which is a feature under Gen head, links NP1 to NP2. The NP1 which occupies the spec of DP originates from the complement of Gen position. The second evidence for the null D head is the construal of bare nouns as either definite, indefinite or generic which are features associated with D. *Ǹkè* seems to be the only overt elements that can occupy the D head position in the Igbo nominal phrase.

References

Abney, Steven P. 1987. *The English noun phrase in its sentential aspect.* PhD dissertation, MIT.

Adger, David. 2003. *Core syntax.* Oxford: Oxford University Press.

Ajíbóyè, Oládiípò. 2007. *The syntax and semantics of Yoruba nominal expressions.* Port Harcourt, Nigeria: M&J Grand Orbit.

Akmajian, Adrian and Frank Heny. 1975. *An introduction to the principles of transformational syntax.* Cambridge, MA: MIT Press.

Amfani, Ahmed H. 1995a. The 'grade' as a functional element and re-interpretation of relations in the Hausa verbal component. In Kola Owolabi (ed.) *Language in Nigeria: Essays in honour of Ayo Bamgbose.* Ibadan: Group Publishers.

Amfani, Ahmed H. 1995b. Double determiner NP constructions in Hausa. In Nolue Emenanjo and Ozo-Mekuri Ndimele (eds.) *Issues in African languages and linguistics: Essays in honour of Kay Williamson.* Aba: NINLAN

Anyanwu, Ogbonna. 2005. *The syntax of Igbo causatives: A minimalist account.* Port Harcourt, Nigeria: M&J Grand Orbit.

Anyanwu, Rose-Juliet. 1996. *Aspects of Igbo grammar.* Beitrage zur Afrikanistik, Band 9.

Bach, Emmon. 1964. *An introduction to transformational grammars.* New York: Holt, Rinehart and Winston.

Bach, Emmon. 1974. *Syntax theory.* New York: Holt, Rinehart and Winston.

Baker, Mark. 1988. *Incorporation: A theory of grammatical function change.* Chicago and London: University of Chicago Press.

Baker, Mark. 2003. *Lexical categories: Verbs, nouns, and adjectives.* Cambridge: Cambridge University Press.

Baltin, Mark and Chris Collins. (eds.) 2001. *The handbook of contemporary syntax theory.* Oxford: Blackwell.

Belletti, Adriana. 2001. Agreement projections. In Baltin, Mark and Chris Collins, 483-510.

Belletti, Adriana and Luigi Rizzi. (eds.) 1996. *Parameters and functional heads: Essays in comparative syntax.* New York: Oxford University Press.

Benmamoun, Elabbas. 2000. *The feature structure of functional categories: A comparative study of Arabic dialects.* New York: Oxford University Press.

Bernstein, Judy. 1997. Demonstratives and reinforcers in Romance and Germanic languages. *Lingua* 102, 87-113.

Bhat, Shankara D.N. 1999. *The prominence of tense, aspect and mood.* Philadelphia: John Benjamins.

Bull, William E. 1963. *Time, tense and the verb*. University of California Publications in Linguistics, 19. Berkeley and Los Angeles: University of California Press.

Cann, Ronnie. 2000. Functional versus lexical: A cognitive dichotomy. *Syntax and semantics 32: The nature and function of syntactic categories*, ed. by Robert Borsley, 37 – 78, New York: Academic Press.

Carnie, Andrew. 2007. *Syntax: A generative introduction 2nd edn*. Oxford: Blackwell Publishing.

Carnochan, J. 1955. An outline analysis of Igbo (a mimeograph).

Carrell, Patricia. 1970. *A transformational grammar of Igbo*. West African Language Monograph series 1, Cambridge: Cambridge University Press.

Chametzky, Robert A. 2000. *Phrase structure: From GB to minimalism*. Oxford: Blackwell.

Chomsky, Noam. 1957. *Syntactic structures*. The Hague: Janua Linguarum 4.

Chomsky, Noam. 1965. *Aspects of the theory of syntax*. Cambridge: MIT Press.

Chomsky, Noam. 1970. Remarks on nominalization. *Readings in English transformational grammar*, ed. by Roderick Jacobs and Peter Rosenbaum, 184-221. Waltham: Ginn.

Chomsky, Noam. 1973. Conditions on transformations. *A festschrift for Morris Halle*, ed. by Stephen Anderson and Paul Kiparsky, 232-86. New York: Holt, Rinehart and Winston.

Chomsky, Noam. 1981. *Lectures on Government and Binding*. Dordrecht: Foris.

Chomsky, Noam. 1986a. *Barriers*. Cambridge, MA: MIT Press.

Chomsky, Noam. 1986b. *Knowledge of language: Its nature, origin and use*. New York: Praeger.

Chomsky, Noam, 1992. A minimalist program for linguistic theory. *MIT occasional papers in linguistics no 1*. Cambridge, MA: MITWPL.

Chomsky, Noam. 1993. A minimalist program for linguistic theory. *The view from building 20: Essays in linguistics in honour of Sylvain Bromberger*, ed. by Kenneth Hale and Samuel J. Keyser, 1-52. Cambridge, MA: MIT Press.

Chomsky, Noam. 1995. *The minimalist program*. Cambridge, MA: MIT Press.

Chomsky, Noam. 2004. Beyond explanatory adequacy. *Cartography of syntactic structure 3: structures and beyond,* ed. by Adriana Belletti 104-131 The Oxford University Press.

Chomsky, Noam and Howard Lasnik. 1977. Filters and control. *Linguistic Inquiry 8*, 425-504.

Chung, Sandra and Alan Timberlake. 1985. Tense, aspect and mood. *Language typology and syntactic description 3: Grammatical categories and the lexicon,* ed. by Timothy Shopen. 202-258. Cambridge: Cambridge University Press.

Cinque, Guglielmo. 2003. *The pronominal origin of relative clauses*. Monograph University of Venice.

Clark, Mary. 1989. *The tonal system of Igbo*. Dordrecht: Foris

Comrie, Bernard. 1976. *Aspect*. Cambridge: Cambridge University Press.

Comrie, Bernard. 1985. *Tense*. Cambridge: Cambridge University Press.

Cowper, Elizabeth. 1992. *A concise introduction to syntactic theory: The Government and Binding approach*. Chicago: University of Chicago Press.

Crystal, David. 1980. *A first dictionary of linguistics and phonetic*s. Boulder, CO: Westview Press.

Crystal, David. 1985. *A dictionary of linguistics and phonetics 2ⁿᵈ edn*. Oxford: Blackwell.

Dahl, Östen. 1979. Typology of sentence negation. *Linguistics 17*, 79-106. Mouton Publishers.

Dahl, Östen. 1985. *Tense and aspect systems*. Oxford: Basil Blackwell.

Davies, Williams and Craig Dresser. 2005. The structure of Javanese and Madurese determiner phrases. *UCLA Working Papers in Linguistics, 21*. 57-71

Dechaine, Rose-Marie. 1993. *Predicates across categories: Towards a category-neutral syntax*. PhD dissertation, University of Massachusetts at Amherst.

Eme, Cecilia A. and Davidson U. Mbagwu. 2009. The Igbo open vowel suffixes. A paper presented at the 23rd Conference of the Linguistic Association of Nigeria, University of Maiduguri, 9-13 November.

Emenanjo, Nwanolue E. 1975. *The Igbo verbal: A descriptive analysis*. M.A. dissertation. University of Ibadan, Nigeria.

Emenanjo, Nwanolue E. 1978. *Elements of modern Igbo grammar*. Ibadan: Oxford University Press.

Emenanjo, Nwanolue E. 1979. On the diachronic aspect of Igbo suffixes. *African Notes 8*. 1: 15-20

Emenanjo, Nwanolue E. 1980. Igbo auxiliaries. A paper given at the Fourth Groningen Round Table on Auxiliaries. University of Groningen.

Emenanjo, Nolue E. 1985. *Auxiliaries in Igbo syntax: A comparative study*. Studies in African Grammatical systems No 2. Indiana University Linguistics Club.

Emonds, Joseph. 1978. The verbal complement of $V' - V$ in French. *Linguistic Inquiry 9*, 151-175.

Emonds, Joseph. 1985. *A unified theory of syntactic categories*. Dordrecht: Foris .

Eze, Ejike. 1995. The forgetten null subject of Igbo. *Theoretical approaches to African linguistics*, ed. by Akinbiyi Akinlabi, 45-81. New Jersey: African World Press.

Fukui, Naoki. 1986. *A theory of category projection and its application*. PhD dissertation, MIT.

Furuya, Kaori. 2008. DP hypothesis for Japanese 'bare' noun phrases. *University of Pennsylvania Working Papers in Linguistics 14.1,* 149-162.

Giorgi, Alessandra and Giuseppe Longobardi. 1991. *The syntax of noun phrases: Configuration, parameters and empty categories*. Cambridge: Cambridge University Press.

Giusti, Giuliana. 1992. Heads and modifiers among determiners: Evidence from Romanian and German. *University of Venice Working Papers in Linguistics 2.1.4*, 1-19.

Green, Margaret M. and G. Egemba Igwe. 1963. *A descriptive grammar of Igbo*. London: Oxford University Press and Berlin: Akademie-Verlag.

Grimshaw, Jane. 1988. Adjuncts and argument structure. *MIT Lexicon Project Working Papers 21*, MIT, Cambridge, MA.

Haegeman, Liliane. 1991. *Introduction to Government and Binding theory*. Cambridge: Cambridge University Press.

Hendrick, Randall. 1991. The morphosyntax of aspect. *Lingua 85*, 171 – 201.

Hockett, Charles. 1958. *A course in modern linguistics*. USA: Macmillan.

Huang, C-T. James. 1995. Logical form. In Welbelhuth, 125 – 75.

Hudson, Richard. 2000. Grammar without functional categories. *Syntax and semantics 32: The nature and function of syntactic categories*, ed. by Robert Borsley, 7 – 36. New York: Academic Press.

Igwe, G. Egemba. 1973. *The role of affixes in Igbo*. London: PhD dissertation, School of Oriental and African Studies, University of London.

Ikegwuonu, Christiana N. 2008. *The structure of Infl phrase in Igbo syntax*. MA Thesis. University of Nigeria, Nsukka.

Ikekeonwu, Clara. 1987. Igbo dialect cluster: A classification. A seminar paper presented to the Department of Linguistics/Nigerian Languages, University of Nigeria, Nsukka.

Jackendoff, Ray. 1972. *Semantic interpretation in generative grammar*. Cambridge, MA: MIT Press.

Jackendoff, Ray. 1977. *X' syntax: A study of phrase structure*. Cambridge, MA: MIT Press.

Jersperson, Otto. 1929. *The philosophy of grammar*. London: Allen and Urwin

Kari Ethelbert E. 2003. *Clitics in Degema: A meeting point of phonology, morphology and syntax*. ILCAA Language Monograph 1. Tokyo: Tokyo University of foreign studies.

Katamba, Francis. 1993. *Morphology*. London: Macmillian.

Katz, Jerrold J. and Paul M. Postal. 1964. *An integrated theory of linguistic description*. Cambridge, MA: MIT Press.

Kayne, Richard 1989. Null subjects and clitic climbing. *The null subject parameter*, ed. by Osvaldo Jaeggli and Kenneth J. Safir. 239 – 261 Dordrecht: Kluwer.

Kayne, Richard. 1994. *The antisymmetry of syntax*. Cambridge, MA: MIT Press.

Kim, Dae-Bin. 1992. *The specificity/Non-specify distinction and scrambling theory.* PhD dissertation, University of Wiscousin, Madison.

Kitagawa, Yoshihisa. 1986. *Subjects in Japanese and English.* PhD dissertation, University of Massachusetts at Amherst.

Klima, Edward S. 1964. Negation in English. *Readings in the philosophy of language: The structure of language,* ed. by Jerrold J. Katz and J.A. Fodor, 246-323. Englewood Cliffs, NJ: Prentice-Hall.

Lasnik, Howard. 1976. Remarks on coreference. *Linguistic Analysis 2,* 1-22.

Lasnik, Howard. 1999. *Minimalist analysis.* Oxford: Blackwell Publishers.

Lasnik, Howard and Juan Uriagereka. 1988. *A course in GB syntax: lectures on binding and empty categories.* Cambridge, MA: MIT Press.

Lasnik, Howard and Juan Uriagereka with Cedrick Boecks 2005. *A course in minimalist syntax.* Oxford: Blackwell Publishers.

Ledgeway, Adam, 2000. *A comparative syntax of the dialects of Southern Italy: A minimalist approach.* Oxford: Blackwell Publishers.

Löbner, Sebastian. 2002. *Understanding semantics.* London: Hodder Arnold

Longobardi, Giuseppe. 2004. The structure of DPs: Some principles, parameters and problems. In Baltin, Mark and Chris Collins, 562-603.

Luraghi, Silvia and Claudia Parodi. 2008. *Key terms in syntax and syntactic theory.* London: Continuum International Publishing Group.

Lyons, John. 1968. *Introduction to theoretical linguistics.* Cambridge: Cambridge University Press.

Mahajan, Anoop K. 1990. *The A/A-bar distinction and movement theory.* PhD dissertation, MIT.

Manfredi, Victor. 1991. *Agbo and Ehugbo: Igbo linguistic consciousness, its origins and limits.* PhD dissertation, Harvard University.

Marantz, Alec. 1995. *The minimalist program.* In Welbelhuth, 351 – 382.

Matthewson, Lisa. 1998. *Determiner systems and quantificational strategies: Evidence from Salish.* The Hague: Holland Academic Graphics.

Mbah, B.M. 1999. *Studies in syntax: Igbo phrase structure.* Nsukka: Prize Publishers

Mbah, B.M. 2006. *GB syntax: Theory and application to Igbo.* Enugu: Association of Nigerian Authors.

Miestamo, Matti. 2005. *Standard negation: The negation of declarative, verbal main clauses in typological perspectives.* Berlin: Walter de Gruyter.

Muysken, Pieter. 2008. *Functional Categories.* Cambridge: Cambridge University Press.

Ndimele, Ozo-mekuri, 1995. On the phonosyntactic dimension of negation. *Issues in African Languages and linguistics: Essays in honour Kay Williamson,* ed. by Nwanolue Emenanjo and Ozo-mekuri Ndimele, 101-116. Aba: National Institute for Nigerian Languages.

Ndimele, Ozo-mekuri. 2004. Negation marking in Igbo. *Language and culture in Nigeria: A festschrift for Okon Essien,* ed. by Ozo-mekuri Ndimele, 939-958. Aba: NINLAN and M&J Grand Orbit.

Ndimele, Ozo-mekuri. 2009. Negation marking in Igbo. *Negation patterns in West African languages and beyond,* ed. by Norbert Cyffer, Erwin Ebermann and Georg Ziegelmeyer, 121-137. Philadelphia: John Benjamins.

Newmeyer, Frederick J. 1986. *Linguistics theory in America.* Orlando: Academic Press.

Nwachukwu, Akụjụọobi P. 1977. Stativity, ergativity and rV suffixes in Igbo. *African languages/Langues Africaines 2,* 119-144

Nwachukwu, Akụjụọobi P. 1985. Inherent complement verbs in Igbo. *Journal of Linguistics Association of Nigeria (JOLAN) 3.*

Nwachukwu, Akụjụọobi P. 1995. *Tone in Igbo syntax.* Nsukka: Igbo Language Association.

Obiamalu, Greg O. 2006. The morphosyntactic spell-out of the functional category neg in Igbo. *Awka Journal of Linguistics 2,* 25 – 36.

Obiamalu, Greg O. 2007. Determiner in the Igbo nominal phrase. *Nigerian languages, literatures, culture and reforms: A festschrift for Ayo Bamgbose,* ed. by Ozo-mekuri Ndimele, 545 – 556. Port Harcourt, Nigeria: Linguistics Association of Nigeria and M & J Grand Orbit.

Obiamalu, Greg O. 2008. Negative-interrogative constructions and tonal prosody in Igbo. *Critical issues in the study of linguistics, languages, and literatures in Nigeria: A festschrift for Conrad Max Benedict Brann,* ed. by Ozo-mekuri Ndimele, Imelda Udoh and Ogbonna Anyanwu, 347-360. Port Harcourt, Nigeria: Linguistics Association of Nigeria and M&J Grand Orbit.

Obiamalu, Greg O. 2009. Agreement by default and v-movement in Igbo. *Language policy, planning and management in Nigeria: A festschrift for Ben Elugbe,* ed. by Ozo-mekuri Ndimele. 917 – 924 Port Harcourt, Nigeria: M&J Grand Orbit.

Obiamalu, Greg O. 2010. On the clitic status of some Igbo subject pronouns. *Journal of the Linguistic Association of Nigeria 13.2,* 301-314

Omamor, Augusta P. 1982. Tense and aspect in Itsekiri. *Journal of West African Languages 12,* 95 – 129.

Ọnụkawa, M. C. 1994. A reclassification of the Igbo =rV suffixes. *Journal of West African Languages 24.2,* 17-29

Ouhalla, Jamal. 1991. *Functional Categories and Parametric variations.* London: Routledge.

Payne, John R. 1992. Negation. *Language typology and syntactic description 3: Grammatical categories and the lexicon,* ed. by Timothy Shopen, 73 – 82, Cambridge: Cambridge University Press.

Pollocks, Jean-Yves. 1989. Verb movement, universal grammar and the structure of IP. *Linguistic Inquiry 20,* 365-424.

Postal, Paul. 1969. On so-called pronouns of English. *Modern studies in English*, ed. by D. Reibel and Sanford Schane. 201-224. Englewood Cliffs NJ: Prentice-Hill.

Progovac, Ljiljana. 1995. Determine phrase in a language without determiners. *University of Venice Working Papers in Linguistics* 5.2, 81-102

Radford, Andrew. 1988. *Transformational grammar.* Cambridge: Cambridge University Press.

Radford, Andrew. 1997. *Syntax: A minimalist introduction.* Cambridge: Cambridge University Press.

Radford Andrew. 2004. *Minimalist syntax: Exploring the structure of English.* Cambridge: Cambridge University Press.

Riemsdijk, Henk van and Edwin Williams. 1986. *Introduction to the theory of grammar.* Cambridge, MA: MIT Press.

Rizzi, Luigi. 1990. *Relativized minimality.* Cambridge, MA: MIT Press.

Ross, John R. 1967. *Constraints on variables in syntax.* PhD dissertation, MIT. Distributed (1968), Bloomington: Indiana University Linguistics Club.

Shlonsky, Ur. 1989. The hierarchical representation of subject-verb agreement. Unpublished manuscript University of Haifa, Israel.

Stowell, Tim. 1981. *Origins of phrase structure.* PhD dissertation, MIT.

Suh, Eugenia. 2005. The nominal phrase in Korean: The role of D in a 'determiner-less' language. *Toronto Working Papers in Linguistics 25.* 10-19

Szabolcsi, Anna. 1987. Functional categories in the noun phrase. *Approaches to Hungarian 2,* ed. by István Kenesei, 167-189. Szeged: Jate

Tallerman, Maggie. 2005. *Understanding syntax 2nd edn.* London: Hodder Arnold.

Travis, Lisa deMena. 1984. *Parameters and effects of word order variation.* PhD dissertation. MIT.

Tsimpli, Iante M. and Jamal Ouhalla. 1990. Functional categories, UG and modularity. Ms, University College and Queen Mary and Westfield College, London.

Ura, Hiroyuki. 2000. *Checking theory and grammatical functions in universal grammar.* Oxford: Oxford University Press.

Uwalaka, Mary-Angela. 1988. *The Igbo verbs: A semantico-syntactic analysis.* Beitrage zur Afrikanistik. (Wien), Band 35, Nr. 48.

Uwalaka, Mary-Angela. 1991. Wh-movement in Igbo. *UCL Working Papers in Linguistics 3,* 185-209

Uwalaka, Mary-Angela. 1997. *Igbo grammar.* Ibadan: Pen Services.

Uwalaka, Mary-Angela. 2003. Tense and v-movement in Igbo. A paper presented at the 4th World Congress of African Linguistics. Rutgers June 17 – 22, 2003.

Welbelhuth, Gert. 1995. X-bar theory and case theory. In Welbelhuth, 3-95.

Welbelhuth, Gert. (ed.) 1995. *Government and binding theory and minimalist program.* Oxford: Blackwell.

Welmers, B.F and W.E. Welmers. 1968. *Igbo: A learner's manual.* A private publication by William E Welmers.

Whorf, Benjamin L. 1938. Some Hopi verbal categories. *Language 14*, 275-86.

Williamson, Kay. 1972. *Igbo-English dictionary.* Benin City: Ethiope Publishing Company.

Williamson, Kay. 1978. Towards a scheme for Igbo verbs. (Manuscript)

Winston, F.D.D. 1973. Polarity, mood and aspect in Ohuhu Igbo verbs. *Africa Language studies 14*: 119 – 79.

Yusuf, Mukhtar A. 1993. *Aspects of the morphosyntax of functional categories in Hausa.* PhD dissertation University of Essex.

Zanuttini, Raffaella. 1996. On the relevance of tense for sentential negation. In Belletti, Adriana and Luigi Rizzi, 181 – 207.

Zubizarreta, Maria Luiza. 1987. *Levels of representation in the lexicon and in the syntax.* Dordrecht: Foris.

Subject Index

Printed in the United States
By Bookmasters